The Measurement Revolution

How To Thrive With Digital Analytics

GREG GUTKOWSKI

TO MY WIFE MONIKA

Special thanks to Nina Fazio for help with copy editing.

CONTENTS

I

Preface

If you recognize any of these frustrations, this book is for you:

- You are unhappy with the quality and integrity of your own business data and information
- You wonder what is worth measuring in your business
- You wonder how much to spend on business analysis in general
- You wonder how the proliferation of cheaper sensors will impact what you can measure and analyze
- You are unhappy with your existing KPIs
- You wonder how to keep up with the latest developments in business analytics
- You wonder how you can keep up with the competition that may be more advanced in data analysis

- You are frustrated with the lack of analytical and data skills among your staff, including senior managers
- You feel that you can no longer run your business on Excel only
- You are frustrated with tech vendor jargon about Big Data, Predictive Analytics, Machine Learning, Artificial Intelligence, Business Intelligence, Data Warehousing, API, and Cloud, among others
- You wonder how more analytics leads to wealth creation
- You sense you need to 'do something about analytics' but don't know where to start

So, what is driving the current measurement revolution? The answer is threefold. It is related to the unprecedented and continuous decrease in the cost of:

1. The measuring equipment itself, including sensors
2. Digital technologies to keep track of the result of the measurement, or recording and transmitting the relevant data
3. Tools to analyze and communicate the measurement results

Measuring more, faster, and better may yield tremendous business benefits, but only if you know when the cost of measurement is less than the benefit of the measurement. This is, in essence, what this book is all about.

1

Introduction

'The best way to predict the future is to digitize it.'

Annie and Jonathan Doe
are happy to announce
the arrival of
Alexis
October 14, 2017
3:15 PM
7 pounds, 6 ounces, 19 inches

We measure from cradle to grave. The first thing reported upon our arrival is the day of the year and the hour of the day we were born. This is accompanied by the measurement of our weight and height, which announces to the world, by proxy, the health of the newborn baby.

The last thing reported about our life is how many years we have managed to live and the value of the assets we left behind. This announces, by proxy, our overall health and success during our earthly activities.

Between the cradle and the grave, we measure years of education, the number of kids, spouses, jobs, houses, cars, and other earthly possessions. We also measure our income, expenses, taxes, and savings. We use some of these measures as scoreboards. Such scoreboards may contribute to our happiness or lack thereof.

However, we found no way to measure happiness. Neither can we measure love, friendship, loyalty, and trust, which reflect the quality of our lives. Consequently, we cannot measure what may matter the most in life.

As groups of humans, we compare our countries, states, cities, and groups on such measurements as income per person, average life expectancy, tax rates, crime rates, and political freedoms, to name a few. We elect politicians based on our feelings and beliefs about what the value of these measures should be.

As a whole civilization, we have been gradually learning to measure various phenomena over the centuries, with most progress being made in the last 200 years.

Science is based exclusively on measurement. We form a hypothesis about the cause and effect of a natural phenomenon and then we experiment with the measurement until we can replicate the results beyond a reasonable doubt - a process that includes a peer review. Thus, no one disputes the law of gravity, for example, and no time is spent debating it.

However, in the social sciences, including economics, business, and marketing, many key drivers of human behavior cannot be measured as effectively and precisely as in pure science. Thus, objectivity is replaced with opinions.

In the 20th century, humans killed between 100 and 200 million of each other in an attempt to convince each other who is right with respect to a hypothesis regarding economic mechanisms supposed to propel the human race. This fight was a function of the lack of objective measures of human progress. If you happened to be on the wrong side of that so-called debate, you and your family ended up killed, or in a labor camp.

In the later part of the same century, we collectively wised up and learned that the free market is the best way to make economic and political progress worldwide. Most countries in the world have made considerable and measurable progress in their standard of living just by following free market principles.

There is a strong correlation between economic freedom, *aka* transparency, and the wealth of societies. For more detailed measurement data and analysis on this topic, see the Economic Freedom Index at https://www.heritage.org/index/.

Is there an ideal free market? No, it does not exist and it will not happen. We are just humans after all.

However, just like in physics, there is the idea of a hypothetical ideal body that does not exist in reality. Nevertheless, it guides the direction of science. A similar concept should guide our business governance; i.e., more objective measurement.

Transparency is sustainable only with good measurements. More analytics - less politics!

The Measurement Revolution

As demonstrated above, the process of measurement is nothing new. We have been measuring countless phenomena for many years in many places. We used measurements in developing international trade as well as in significant progress in the sciences.

Few would argue that the great progress that humanity achieved in the last 200 years would be possible without a well thought out system of measurements.

So, what is driving the current measurement revolution? The answer is threefold. It is related to the unprecedented and continuous decrease in the cost of:

1. The measuring equipment itself (this includes sensors)
2. Methods of keeping track of the results of the measurement, or recording and transmitting the relevant data
3. Tools for analyzing and communicating the measurement results

The cost of collecting, storing, and analyzing data has decreased about 10,000 times over the last 20 years! I know of no comparable phenomena in the history of humans, whereby the cost of comparable power is decreasing at such an astonishing rate. In addition, technology experts agree that this trend of lower technology prices will last at least another 20 years.

Therefore, we can measure, record, analyze, and communicate at rapidly decreasing costs at a rate never experienced in human history. This leads to two major benefits:

1. Measuring phenomena that existed before but have never been measured
2. Measuring more frequently and precisely the manual processes that existed before

Benefit Type 1
Measuring For The First Time

Market Research

Twenty years ago, there was no way to count how many times people searched for the best barbeque grill before they decided to purchase one. Today, Google records every instance of every phrase typed into the Google search box by anyone in the world, with a detailed breakdown by city, date, and demographics. This may not be important to you personally, but it's very important to the producer of barbeque grills trying to estimate the demand for their products over the next 12 months in Florida versus Minnesota.

Effectiveness Of Advertising

Traditional advertising was very hard to measure with respect to its effectiveness. It is almost impossible to determine how many gadgets advertised on multiple roadside billboards are sold as a result of such advertising.

It's still hard to determine which ad is responsible for a sale, but we have made great progress on this front. Actually, the fortunes of Google and Facebook are directly tied to the fact that advertising became more precise, traceable, and attributable. Advertisers finally found a way to better target and measure the success of online advertising campaigns.

If one clicks on a webpage ad and then buys the advertised product online within a few minutes of seeing that ad, there is 99% certainty which particular ad led to a particular sale.

As a result, in the U.S. over $50 billion a year is spent on online advertising, with most proceeds going to the Google-Facebook oligopoly. For the sake of comparison, traditional cable TV ad spending is about the same. The spending on radio ads is about $15 billion a year.

GPS

Another example is GPS recording our geographical coordinates every second. Hence, we know where we are, we know the optimal way to go, and we can estimate how long it will take to get to the destination. Thirty years ago, everyone carried a lot of maps in their glove compartments. A lot of turns and exits were missed while driving. How many paper maps have you seen lately?

GPS brings tremendous value to businesses that operate fleets of cars or trucks. It is now possible to account for every car or truck all over the country and to be able to optimize their routes— thus shortening delivery cycles, saving on fuel, and better avoiding driver fatigue.

The third example in this category is wildlife tracking with GPS collars to better understand the behavior of a species and thus to better manage our natural resources. Or to track our puppy Fido who wanders away occasionally.

Drones

Speaking of tracking, drones provide a completely new way to survey land for agriculture, construction, and real estate. A great example is a drone-based service monitoring for cracks in large and tall structures such as antennas, bridges, or skyscrapers with the capability of distinguishing old peeling paint from the beginnings of possible structural damage. In the not so distant past, the cost of such monitoring was prohibitive as it would require using expensive helicopters and their crews.

In the not so distant past, we could not analyze DNA, as the cost of computing was prohibitive. Today, we can order an analysis of our genome for less than $1,000. Such analysis can help to detect and fight a mortal health problem.

Benefit Type 2
Measuring More Frequently And Granularly

Automation And Optimization

Manufacturing processes have existed for many years, but they were not always measured, controlled, automated, and optimized to the extent possible today.

A great example here is the fully controlled, mostly automated, and highly optimized production assembly of modern cars. Today, Smart produces about 100 cars per employee per year. In the 1930s, Ford built 10 cars per employee per year. Keep in mind that Smart is much more complex when compared to 1930s-era Ford. Thus, automation and optimization made possible by better measurement led to a more than 10-fold increase in worker productivity in less than 90 years.

A similar rate of automation and optimization can be seen in electrical power generation.

Another example is the almost fully automated production of soft drinks and beer, including bottling, packaging, and warehousing.

Telemedicine

Inexpensive portable or wearable equipment that can measure vital signs such as heart rate, blood pressure, number of steps walked, body mass index, or sugar level, and transmit the results to a health provider via a smartphone is now available for less than $300 dollars. It can be used on a continuous daily basis for a very low fixed cost.

In the past, a patient had to travel to a medical facility to get simple vitals taken. This involved scheduling an appointment, waiting, and filling out a lot of forms. In other words, it was expensive, time consuming, and inconvenient. Thus, it was done infrequently and sometimes only when the patient was already in trouble. Preventive measurements were just cost prohibitive.

More frequent and very inexpensive home monitoring of vital signs is already driving down readmission rates after major surgeries and is being used in programs to prevent diabetes, heart disease, or obesity. When implemented consistently on a large scale, it has the potential to drive down the cost of healthcare by 50%. I know of no better example of the impact on our civilization that is related to more frequent and less expensive measurement than this use for monitoring vital signs.

Social Interactions - Emails, Calls, Texts, And Posts

People have always been interacting socially. However, for most, the radius of their interaction was limited to about 15 miles from the place where they were born. Travel was very expensive and unaffordable for most. For those in urban areas, the interaction may have been daily. For those in rural areas, a little time after weekly church service was the major interaction time. Thus, the spread of news, innovations, and ideas was going at a relatively slow pace.

Compare it now with instant communication via text, emails, and social media. It is frequent, carries no cost, and does not limit one to a 15-mile radius. The number and type of interactions is easily measured and can be used to shape communication campaigns worldwide. Top celebrities may have over 50 million followers on social media worldwide.

We know what messages were sent, who got them, who responded or who did not and in what way over any period of time.

As a result, ideas and innovations now travel across the world in no time and at very little or no cost. Like any other technology, it may be used for noble or nefarious purposes, but there is no question about the increased efficiency and effectiveness of global communication and hence the spread of innovation.

Online Education

In the past, a teacher was limited with respect to the number of quizzes or tests one could grade. Grading student work by hand is very time consuming. Thus, grading was infrequent and seldom tied to the learning style or disabilities of students.

Enter online education where thousands of students can be automatically and instantly graded after taking a test online. Feedback is instant and specific. The time allowed to answer a question may vary by a student's abilities with more time allowed for those who are visually, hearing, or otherwise impaired.

Thus, more frequent and more granular checks and feedback on student progress is now feasible at a lower cost. This may contribute to a higher quality of learning and higher teacher productivity.

It is worth noting that the measurement of social interactions and education effectiveness can be very relevant to the productivity of business employees. We can closely guide, coach, and monitor their communication and provide continuous learning. These are major levers of increased business productivity today.

Smart Cities - Logistics & Transportation

We are seeing considerable progress in the ability to measure real traffic patterns today. Most drivers carry smartphones. Each smartphone has a unique MAC address that can be traced by Bluetooth type roadside sensors without the knowledge of the vehicle's owner. The MAC address identifies the device but does not carry the user's private data. In other words, it can be used to track a vehicle as an anonymous unit, which is enough for the purpose of traffic control and optimization.

Thus, it is possible to account for most traffic given a sufficient number of Bluetooth roadside sensors.

The next logical step is to use this information to plan road expansions, reroute traffic during emergencies, and optimize street lights to assure the continuous and smooth flow of vehicles to reduce gas consumption, congestion, and pollution. All of these benefits are directly tied to the ability to track vehicle movement at a high degree of precision in terms of time and space.

Sports

Last but not least, we will discuss the impact of better measurements in sports. Given the amount of money and attention devoted to sports, it is a worthy pursuit from the profit perspective. More frequent measurement can also impact athletes' health and performance.

The concept is similar to telemedicine, but expanded beyond vital signs. Each athlete can be monitored multiple times daily with respect to all possible activities including vitals and nutrition. The data can then be correlated with performance data during a specific event and used to coach, improve, optimize, etc.

Sports analytics is a fast-growing field because there is demonstrable proof that more frequent and more granular measurements and analysis are beneficial.

Additional Benefit: Increased Transparency

It's our strong belief that more measurements are catalysts for increased transparency, and thus lead to greater accountability and trust in business, politics, education, news, nonprofits, sports, entertainment, health care, politics, and the government. This is one of the greatest benefits of the trend toward more frequent and more granular digital measurement.

Trust, in addition to its moral dimension, also has a very beneficial practical aspect; that is, it lowers the cost of doing business. It's obvious that the more people trust each other, the more productive and the longer their collaborations will thrive. The more people trust each other, the less time and energy is spent on lawyers, arbiters, forensic accountants— and watching their own backs.

No Free Ride

It's worth noting that the benefit of measuring can materialize only when the cost of measuring is less than the benefit of measuring itself. The following quote perfectly depicts this quandary: "Not everything that counts can be counted, and not everything that can be counted counts." We don't know for sure who said that, but it's frequently attributed to William Bruce Cameron or Albert Einstein.

The digital revolution provides great measurement tools, but they do not substitute for thinking, sound judgment, and common sense. It is the job of management to decide what and how frequently to measure with respect to key business processes and how to reward teams for practicing the art of measurement in day-to-day operations. That job is not easy in the context of rapid decreases in the cost of measurement. Every day may bring a new opportunity to measure faster, cheaper, and better to increase profits. However, watching these trends could be a full time job by itself.

Digital Revolution Or Measurement Revolution

One may wonder if the digital revolution led to the measurement revolution or the other way around. I believe that the tremendous increase in the power of hardware and software is just a catalyst for progress. In other words, it is necessary but not a sufficient component of the progress of civilization. Technological infrastructure is of no value unless it leads to better processes and outcomes. In other words, the full benefit of technological changes will only be possible when we fully leverage our ability to measure more frequently and more granularly.

Even this is not sufficient. We need to be able to analyze these measures and take action based on the results. Nevertheless, without the right measurements, the whole discussion is moot.

History Of Measurement

One of the oldest measures is **length**. The inch reflects the length of a thumb. The foot is self-explanatory. Yard comes from two lengths of a forearm. The mile relates to the Roman *mille passus* which translates to a thousand paces.

To standardize the measure of length, the concept of a standard cubit was adopted. It was originally based on the length of a forearm and a standard length rod was kept in the temples of Mesopotamia and Egypt. It was used to sell commodities by length and to survey land.

Weight measurement originated by using a number of grains of wheat as an equivalent.

Volume measurement started with baskets, sacks, or jars in standard sizes.

For most of history, humans had **no** notion of hours, minutes, or seconds. A day, night, forenoon, and afternoon were sufficient to measure **time**. The clockwork was invented in the 14th century and introduced the concept of dividing the day into 12 hours.

Atmospheric pressure measurement dates back to the mid 17th century. The first thermometer arrived at the beginning of the next century with significant contributions from Fahrenheit and Celsius.

The first chronometer was built in 1735. This device, later referred to as a clock, allowed us to precisely measure elapsed **time** while sailing the oceans—the fundamental requirement for navigation when combined with a sextant measuring the angle between to visible objects.

Until the 18th century, there was no unified measurement system used among various countries. The variety of units made consistent comparisons very laborious. This contributed to fraud and errors in commercial transactions and also slowed trade and scientific progress.

With the expansion of world trade, there was a need for international standards. France led the way by adopting the decimal metric system in 1837. Since then, most countries comply with the International System of Units (SI) definitions of seven base units of measurement:

Length	meter
Mass	kilogram
Time	seconds
Electric current	ampere
Temperature	kelvin
Amount of substance	mole
Luminous intensity	candela

It is interesting to note that the international community has agreed to these scientific measurement standards, but not to the standard measure of wealth. Some countries have tried to peg their currencies to a unit of gold. However, most politicians found that it constrained their power, and such a standard is not likely to be adopted again anytime soon.

In practical terms, the U.S. dollar is being used as a common international measure reflecting the wealth of the economy. Nevertheless, the lack of an underlying gold standard opens it to the criticism of imprecision related to the political imbalance of power reflected in monetary and inflation policies, also known as the unaccountable printing of money.

In this book, we will concentrate on business productivity measurements such as output per

time, cost per unit, return on investment, elapsed time, etc. Please note that all the business process measures are derivatives of the seven basic units of measurement plus the units of currency. Examples include the length of time and amount of electricity required to produce a ton of output, or the amount of volume produced per second per employee or shift. Other examples reflect the measurement of productivity in terms of money and include profit or loss per product, customer, employee, etc.
I strongly believe that there is a lot of progress to be made to enhance our measurement systems.

However, I am also very aware that such systems need to be guided by values that are sometimes impossible to measure. Hence, the job of managers is safe forever; someone will have to make these value judgment calls and be accountable to stakeholders.

Therefore, following is a collection of my favorite quotes regarding measuring what may not be measurable:

"The single best machine to **measure** trust is a human being. We haven't figured out a metric that works better than our own sort of, like, 'There's something fishy about you.'" (Simon Sinek)

"You can **measure** opportunity with the same yardstick that measures the risk involved. They go together." (Earl Nightingale)

"As to the evil which results from a censorship, it is impossible to **measure** it, for it is impossible to tell where it ends." (Jeremy Bentham)

"I don't **measure** America by its achievement but by its potential." (Shirley Chisholm)

"The **measure** of who we are is what we do with what we have." (Vince Lombardi)

"We are a people unafraid to welcome 'your tired, your poor, your huddled masses', because we **measure** others by the quality of their hopes for the future, not by the circumstances of their birth." (Blase J. Cupich)

"If Jeff Bezos and I had started Amazon.com in a poverty-stricken corner of Africa, there would have been no job creation because there would be no people to buy the stuff from Amazon.com. The difference here is the American middle class, which is by every **measure** the most extraordinary economic achievement in the history of the world." (Nick Hanauer)

"I believe you accomplish what you **measure**." (Stacy Brown-Philpot)

"eBay's business is based on enabling someone to do business with another person, and to do that, they first have to develop some **measure** of trust, either in the other person or the system." (Pierre Omidyar)

"The most interesting thing about the idea of money is that it makes it possible to **measure** something in previous ages we couldn't be sure about, and that something is power." (Daniel Keys Moran)

"You **measure** a government by how few people need help." (Patricia Schroeder)

"If you cannot **measure,** you cannot manage." (Anonymous)

"Nobody should try to use data unless he has collected data." (W. Edwards Deming)

"In God we trust, all others bring data." (Warren C. Tyner, Chief engineer of Ford Motor Company)

"Without data you're just another person with an opinion." (Anonymous)

"The most important figures that one needs for management are unknown or unknowable, but successful management must nevertheless take account of them." (Lloyd S. Nelson, director of statistical methods for the Nashua Corporation)

"Man is the **measure** of all things." (Protagoras 485-411 BC)

"The **measure** of success is happiness and peace of mind." (Bobby Davro)

"Action is the real **measure** of intelligence." (Napoleon Hill)

"The **measure** of a man is what he does with power." (Plato)

"But the person who scored well on an SAT will not necessarily be the best doctor or the best lawyer or the best businessman. These tests do not **measure** character, leadership, creativity, perseverance." (William Julius Wilson)

"The SAT is not perfect. We all know smart, knowledgeable people who do badly on standardized tests. But neither is it useless. SAT scores do **measure** both specific knowledge and valuable thinking skills." (Virginia Postrel)

"We shouldn't **measure** everything in terms of GDP figures or economics. There is something called quality of life." (Nigel Farage)

"Ugliness is the **measure** of imperfection." (H. G. Wells)

"Simplicity and repose are the qualities that **measure** the true value of any work of art." (Frank Lloyd Wright)

"In the state of nature, profit is the **measure** of right." (Thomas Hobbes)

"Although we take it for granted, sanitation is a physical **measure** that has probably done more to increase human life span than any kind of drug or surgery." (Deepak Chopra)

"Success has always been easy to **measure**. It is the distance between one's origins and one's final achievement." (Michael Korda)

"Your conscience is the **measure** of the honesty of your selfishness. Listen to it carefully." (Richard Bach)

2

Why Analytics and Why Now?

Let's start this section with the definition of analysis:

Analysis is the process of breaking a complex topic or substance into smaller parts in order to gain a better understanding of it.

In a nutshell, analysis is the process of understanding how things work in life, family, engineering, business, science, politics, entertainment, etc.

The underlying idea is to discover, understand, and be able to communicate what was the cause and what was the effect.

The idea is very simple but the application can be very complex. It is simple where cause and effect are closely tied, easy to observe, and made up of few factors.

From Simple To Complex

Thus, it's not hard to analyze what might have caused a low balance in your checking account if you are the only one who controls it, you have only one source such as regular wage income via direct deposit, and you use electronic payments and little cash. Eyeballing your monthly statement will be more than sufficient.

The problem is much more complex if you manage cash flow for a multinational business with a multitude of banks, various accounts, exchange rates, payments, debt repayment schedules, payrolls, etc. This could be a full time work for a team of accountants.

At least with money, the analysis could be conclusive thanks to double-entry accounting systems. Given enough time, one can find out what caused the low balance at any given point in time.

In science, things get more complex as the causes can be interrelated and not easily observed or measured. One of the best examples is the law of physics. In many instances, both causes and effects are hard to measure, yet they are proven to work according to proven formulas. Examples include Newton's law of universal gravitation,

$$F = G \frac{m_1 m_2}{r^2}$$

where F is the gravitational force acting between two objects, m_1 and m_2 are the masses of the objects, r is the distance between the centers of their masses, and G is the gravitational constant.

Here again, it was genius of Newton to formulate a hypothesis for why an apple would fall to the ground. It was a scientific achievement to have it measured and proven. Nevertheless, once it was proven, no one disputed it anymore as the measurements are easy to repeat.

A similar process is applicable to most chemical reactions; i.e., we know what ingredients in what quantities, under what conditions (pressure and/or temperature) will result in the creation of a new substance.

The situation gets much more complex when the components that cause the effect are not easily measurable or not measurable at all.

Murder, She Wrote

Newton's scientific genius may not have been applicable in the analysis of a murder mystery, for example. Few things can be measured with respect to the motive of a murderer. Even knowing the motive and proving it in a court of law can be two different things. Was the victim killed for money, mercy, convenience, or jealousy? No one will ever be able to measure it, yet it can be discerned, understood, and even proven.

Business analysis could be equally complex as it is usually made up of the two sets of components discussed above: measurable and unmeasurable.

Consumers' tastes, preferences, incomes, motivations, and behaviors are very hard or impossible to measure, understand, and document. Yet, they are the major drivers of our economy, which is closely tied to consumption. On the other hand, businesses can measure the inputs, outputs, capital, and time to produce, distribute, and sell their goods.

In this book we will concentrate on the analysis of the latter phenomena; i.e., things that we can measure and explain with indisputable business data. The former is the domain of sociologists, psychologists, and psychiatrists. But let's not forget that when analyzing marketing results, we will have to accept a high degree of ambiguity and many times admit that we do not really know 100% why we failed or succeeded. Such ambiguity contributes to the high risk of new marketing initiatives and also partially explains the very high level of business failures, especially during the initial years of operation.

Yes, luck still is a very important ingredient in marketing. We can minimize risk, but we can't eliminate unknowns completely.

More Data Is Being Collected

We collect more data than ever before. Actually, we double the amount of data collected year. It is expected that in less than five years, we will be doubling the amount of data collected every month!

Over ninety percent of the data in the world today has been created in the last two years alone.

What is driving such an astonishing trend? The answer is related to the ease and low cost of collection driven by less expensive hardware and software.

Digital Footprint

Facebook and Google have over a billion active users daily. All the social media activities plus searches and emails generate tremendous amounts of data being generated, transmitted, and stored.

Online advertising driven by the above is another contributor to a lot of the data being generated.

Electronic payments via smartphones, credit cards, direct transfers, or any other electronic form contribute to that amount as well. With the growing trend toward electronic payments and with the growing affluence of the world's population buying even more, there is no end in sight to this trend. Even cash payments are mostly digitally recorded by point of sales (POS) systems today.

E-commerce applications generate a lot of data as visitors fill out forms, order items, and make payments.

- websites
- social media
- online advertising
- smartphone apps
- Internet of Things apps

Supply Chain

The supply chain, or the mechanism used to move parts, components, and final product around the world, requires a lot of detailed tracking.

A lot of tracking is driven by less expensive sensors, which send even more data more frequently.

In general, as the world specializes, there is a growing need to move parts, ideas, sales, and money around. Thus we have more suppliers than ever. A case in point is iPhone production. Today, it involves 189 suppliers in 789 locations worldwide. It is worth noting that none of the manufacturing facilities are owned by Apple. Now imagine the amount of data that needs to be exchanged to coordinate all these activities.

For comparison, in 2001, seventy-five percent of Nokia phone parts were made in eight Nokia factories and mostly in one country, Finland.

- More suppliers due to worldwide specialization
- The iPhone has 189 suppliers with 789 locations, none owned by Apple
- In 2001, 75% of Nokia phones made in Nokia factories

Global Competition

Worldwide markets for lots of products and services introduced more international competition. Today, we not only compete with other U.S.-based companies. We compete worldwide with giants from Europe, China, Japan, and India, among others.

There is more upside associated with the right decision and the right management. In other words, the reward is commensurate with global domination, not just the national one.

Conversely, there is more downside associated with missing global trends and/or poor decision-making.

- More competition globally
- More upside with right decisions
- More downside with missed trends

More Regulations

As the world grows more complex, we're seeing increased regulation on many business fronts. This includes compliance with environmental, safety, medical, financial, and transportation regulations, among others.

Just recently, for example, a new regulation was issued in the U.S. to oversee the number of hours driven by truckers during the day. The limit is ten, and it is tracked electronically in real time. Imagine the amount of the data this will generate.

The trend toward unified patient medical records with associated security and privacy regulations will also contribute to more data being collected.

The trend toward more transparency in finance will also contribute much more data being collected and stored for long periods of time.

- More regulations
- Compliance - medical
- Compliance - financial

Increased Cost Of Labor

While technology prices are going down, the price of labor is going up around the world. It may not be going up at the same rate in all markets, but it is and will be growing everywhere. Thus, it makes perfect sense to substitute expensive labor with digital analysis, automation, and better digital tools in general.

It seems like a logical solution, yet it is not easy to implement. Historically, we have not developed a lot of analytical, digital, and software skills as they were of less relevance and importance.

Given the rapid changes in technology, our educational systems have not been able to react fast enough. Today, you may find a financial executive with thirty years of experience, but there is no one with the same tenure in digital marketing because the field of digital advertising is less than ten years old.

As a result of all the trends discussed above, we are experiencing a simultaneous increase in demand for analytical skills with the shortage of such skills. If there is a limit to digital progress, it is in the lack of skills to take advantage of all the benefits associated with it.

To a certain extent, rapid digital progress took many businesses by surprise and most are in the process of learning how to adapt to it.

- Increased demand for analytical skills
- Shortage of skills
- Not in demand before
- Schools need to catch up

Summary

At the same time, analytics have never been so affordable and valuable. The sensors and software are omnipresent, much less expensive, and much easier to operate. The cost of storing data is negligible. However, unless digital technologies are deployed to solve the right problem, it's a waste of time and resources.

Therefore, to take full advantage of the digital progress, one needs to combine sound business judgment with the best business processes and the best digital tools and analytics. Digital technologies by themselves are not going to solve many problems as they are only tools. It's the job of management to determine what tools are relevant and how they should be used.

Analytical systems more affordable

- Sensors
- Software
- Storage
- Data transmission
- Software easier to use
- Knowledge of business process

3

Measurement Value Chain

Let me introduce the concept of the Measurement Value Chain. The remainder of this book will be mostly based on this logical model.

The Measurement Value Chain is made up of four interlocking components:

- Data
- Information
- Knowledge
- Wisdom

Like any chain, the strength of the whole is a function of the weakest link.

Data

In a general sense, data are the raw numbers in a spreadsheet or database. Data could also be a separate standalone image with no description. Or a single video or Twitter post with no context. It could be a series of numbers jotted down by hand on a napkin in a coffee shop.

Data are granular, atomic facts that form the basis for reasoning or calculation. Data can come in a variety of traditional and digital formats.

As a global humanity, we double the amount of stored digital data every twelve months! We already discussed the major drivers behind this phenomenon in the previous sections of this book.

Data by itself is of little value. The metaphor here could be a set of bricks or Lego™ blocks. Until they are put together in some kind of structure, whether a building or a toy, they have little relevance by themselves. Yet, they are the chunks or pieces of something bigger.

Information

Information is born when raw, granular data is summarized in a table or graph chart. Thus, a financial report, sales history graph, or inventory levels shown on a screen shot are pieces of information. So are the images supporting such information. A good example here is a picture of a damaged car with the corresponding estimate in dollars to get it fixed as part of an insurance claim.

What is interesting is that information by itself is still not enough to impact decision-making unless it gets into the hands of a person who knows how to interpret it and what to do with it. If you got a financial statement from an anonymous company, would you know what it means? Not even the most experienced CFO could use such information without additional context. If you got the MRI results of a patient, would you know what to do with this medical information? Even the most experienced MD may have trouble making a diagnosis without knowing the other basic vital signs of the patient.

Knowledge

Information becomes knowledge when it's analyzed and interpreted in the context of experience or information that may not be available online or in print, but is instrumental in drawing conclusions. In most cases this context is the professional experience of the person doing the interpretation.

Our professional experiences reside in our brains and we are far from being able to store all the experience needed for sound decision-making in a computer database. Even if we could, there is no substitute for the human brain as far as the best analytical tool ever invented. Complex business analysis will never be automated because it involves too many unstructured elements that can't be digitally connected by even the most powerful computer.

One example is awareness of the surrounding cultural context in decision-making. One needs to know, for example, that in India, the color white is associated with mourning, while in the U.S. it accompanies weddings. Or in Japan, various colors depict the steps of societal hierarchy.

Another example is company culture, which may be very different depending on the age of the top manager or the sources of funding. One will use very different approaches with respect to a privately-owned company run by a 70-year-old as compared to a publicly funded company run by a newly appointed millennial.

Actually, the awareness of various cultures and sub-cultures is extremely important in marketing segmentation and in business in general. Many consumer product companies live or die by the right assessment of various consumer behaviors based on their ages, incomes, geographies, and education levels, to name a few.

Think how many genres of music we have—at least twenty. There is no single music group that spans them all, and not a single person I know is an exclusive fan of only one genre. Think how much money a music group could make by catering to the right subculture—or lose, if they bet on reggae vs. heavy metal or country, for example.

Wisdom

And finally, all the knowledge in the world is useless unless it's translated into action based on that knowledge. We call it wisdom.

Wisdom is defined here as the soundness of an action in the context of knowledge, experience, and judgment. It is also called decision-making.

Please note that not every decision made has been wise. However, every wise decision must have been based on sound knowledge, experience, and good judgment.

One of the reasons for high executive pay is that good decision-making is a very hard and stressful job. First, you have to possess a lot of knowledge, experience, and good judgment. These three components exist quite rarely in one person. And such a person would need to possess the mental endurance to cope with the risk of making such decisions. Top executives make decisions that affect their own professional lives as well as thousands of their employees and business partners. It is not easy to manage so much pressure.

On top of all this, as we discussed before, because of global competition, the cost of making a wrong decision is very high. So is the reward for a good one. Thus, I can foresee top executive compensation increasing even further. This is similar to the phenomenon in professional sports where a star athlete is paid hundreds of millions of dollars per year more than a teammate who is average but still very good.

Visit A Doctor

Let me illustrate the concept of the Measurement Value Chain in the context of a visit to a doctor.

Let's say a parent brings in a toddler who is coughing and running a fever.

First, the doctor will start collecting all the data by asking questions of the parents and ordering various tests that will provide raw data points.

Data from various tests and parental testimony will be transferred to charts and tables, compared with other data in the system, such as historical data, to check if this happened before and to what extent. This will become information.

This assumes, however, that all the relevant data is in the database. This may not be the case when a child has moved between two doctors who do not share the same healthcare databases (which is the majority of cases in the U.S. today).

Thus, the doctor will look at this data and, based on his medical knowledge and the child's physical exam, may diagnose a common cold. In medicine, in many cases, the doctor may not have all the necessary information for the right diagnosis and some degree of guessing is involved. Cold symptoms may be identical to symptoms of other diseases...

Such a diagnosis would be a worthless experience if the doctor didn't write the prescription for the right medicine.

Now it's the parents' turn to act: go to a pharmacy, get the prescription filled, and give the medicine to the child. This is called *action based on knowledge*.

In many cases, physicians warn their patients' parents to finish the medicine, even if the symptoms go away. In many cases, parents don't follow this advice due to overconfidence after the child is feeling better. If they do not, the whole effort could have been in vain and such decision-making could not qualify as wisdom.

So, to summarize, we may have had perfect data, information, and knowledge, yet the unsoundness of a wrong action may wipe out the whole preceding effort.

In business decision-making, the situation described above is quite common. The actual decision-making and/or a lack of consistent implementation may be the weakest link in the Measurement Value Chain.

Case Study

Let's apply this model to an Internet marketing campaign, where the data will be stored in Google Analytics and other social media analytics databases.

It will become information when we chart it, compare it to other values, determine trends, etcetera.

Without an intimate knowledge of the business at hand, it would be very hard to turn this information into knowledge. We may wonder why Facebook *likes* did not turn into to website visits or purchases.

We need to call a 'doctor'—somebody whose experience and knowledge of the business will lead us to the right conclusions. The 'doctor'—or an experienced digital marketer—will explain that someone *liking* and buying from them may not be related. For example, you may be getting a lot of *likes* from existing customers that have already bought from you with no intention to buy more in the near future.

It's impossible to store all information relevant to business analysis in one homogenous database. For example, in cases such as natural disasters, bankruptcy of a supplier, election results, or changes in currency exchange rates, it's hard to imagine fully automated decisions anytime soon.

The same goes for regional differences in food or fashion. It's hard to imagine a lot of demand today for boiled peanuts outside of the American south, or for grey only toys for kids anywhere in the world. These rules are not codified anywhere, yet they are usually known by experienced marketers.

In addition, many businesses offer highly complex products and services, and it's impossible to market them effectively without knowing how they work. And how they work is not codified either. Sometimes even product designers cannot explain their own products. This is why we have so many videos on 'How to use XYZ' on YouTube.

So, despite all the hype about artificial intelligence, I cannot imagine marketing being done by machines as long as humans are around. To move from information to knowledge, you need intervention by an experienced human being.

To make things even more complex, people with knowledge may not have the authority to take action. This is a very common phenomenon, especially in larger organizations where an experienced analyst is not an executive and cannot make financial decisions. The analyst can only recommend the desired action to higher authority.

In such cases, the effectiveness of a marketing campaign will also depend on the degree of communication and cooperation between the analyst and an executive.

The table below depicts the complexity of the actual implementation of an integrated online system performing all these analyses in real time.

Metrics	Data Source	Comments
Social media shares, friends, followers	Twitter, Facebook, LinkedIn	Hard to automate, usually done by hand
Open rate, click rate, new email signups	Email systems	How to reconcile
Return visits	Google Analytics	
New visitors	Google Analytics	
Inbound links	Google Search Console	
Time on site	Google Analytics	
Number of leads	Google Analytics and/or CRM	Transfer by hand between Google Analytics and CRM
Order, repeat orders	Google Analytics, ERP, ordering system	Cart abandonment analysis needed
Sales	Google Analytics, CRM, ERP	
Revenues, average order	CRM/ERP	
Customer referrals	CRM	If collected there

It looks like, under the best-case scenario, we need to deal with six separate systems to get all the right data!

- Social media
- Email
- Google Analytics
- Webmaster Tools
- In-house CRM
- ERP systems

And then we have to put it into a single database and provide reporting and analytical tools to turn this data into meaningful information.

To provide meaningful information for decision-making, we have to prepare, at a minimum, a report as presented below.

	Variance	Plan	Actual
Visits	3%	1,200,000	1,241,000
Engagements	9%	60,000	65,176
Conversions	19%	3,450	4,112
Expenses	-4%	$300,000	$287,000
Revenue	15%	$567,989	$654,782
Profit	37%	$267,989	$367,782

The first column shows categories of information such as visits, engagements, and conversions as well as the corresponding expenses, revenues, and profits for a digital marketing campaign. The remaining columns show the plan, actual, and variance values for each.

Now we understand why it's so hard to come up with such a simple report online in real time. In addition to relying on multiple data sources, we also have to make sure that the right costs are allocated among the right channels, which by itself is not always simple.

However, the lack of an automated version of this report leads to a lot of time spent on the manual compilation of data and report generation, or it results in failing to understand where the profits are coming from. Either way, without such an analysis, we can't take advantage of the single best benefit of digital marketing: transparent return on investment.

How Strong Is The Chain?

We mentioned that the Measurement Value Chain is a logical concept based on the idea of an interlocking continuum. And as with any chain, the weakest link determines its strength.

Thus, the more links we have, the more important it is to keep them at equal strength. But how do we compare the strength of our data quality with our analytical skills or the quality of decision-making? In the 'How To Measure Your Business' chapter, I present the methodology to achieve just that.

The idea is to assess the overall strength of the corporate Measurement Value Chain first. Then we need to concentrate on the weakest links, while working on the improvement of the overall strength of our corporate analytical capabilities.

4

Value of Information and Knowledge

According to the U.S. Department of Commerce, in 2017, only thirty percent of Gross National Product was attributable to industries with tangible physical processes and outputs.

https://www.bea.gov/industry/gdpbyind_data.htm

These include:

- Agriculture
- Forestry
- Manufacturing
- Mining
- Construction
- Transportation and Warehousing

The rest of our wealth was tied to various services including financial, healthcare, government, information technologies, management, and education.

Thus we can conclude that over seventy percent of our national income is tied directly to knowledge and not necessarily to our combined production of physical assets.

Thus, it comes at no great surprise that Google, Facebook, Apple, Amazon, and Microsoft are among the top ten largest public companies not only in the U.S. but in the world. All these companies provide data and information. But please keep in mind that they do not provide knowledge as defined earlier. Actually, all information technology products and services are useless until they are effectively incorporated into business processes, including effective decision-making.

Let's examine the value of information, or lack of it, in key human activities, not limited to business only.

Military Intelligence

Wars are won on intelligence and logistics. Intelligence is needed to assess the likelihood of being attacked and/or likelihood of winning.

The whole idea of global diplomacy is based on countries' gathering relevant intelligence on each other, thus decreasing the likelihood of a major conflict.

Nevertheless, when conflict arises, the value of intelligence may make the difference between victory and defeat. Breaking the secret Enigma code of Hitler's military communications had a significant impact on the end of World War II.

Breaking the code of the Soviet's Red Army in 1920 saved Western Europe from communist invasion.

Thus, as taxpayers, few mind funding CIA, military, and State Department intelligence-gathering around the world. It is worth noting that each country is involved in hacking each other's computer systems for the sole purpose of gaining military and/or industrial advantage. In the long run, industrial advantage turns into a military one.

It can be said that our freedom is guarded by the quality of the data and information we collect. The Measurement Value Chain model is relevant here as well. We need experienced intelligence data analysts to provide information to decision-makers—in this case our political and military leaders who will decide what action, if any, to take on such information.

Healthcare

In healthcare today, poor patient records contribute to a top cause of wrongful deaths in the U.S.—approximately 250,000 per year. That number is bigger than all deaths from suicides, homicides, and car accidents combined!

As the majority of health records are either on paper or stored in multiple inaccessible databases, physicians can make decisions based on wrong or insufficient information. The information and data could just be missing, or it could be incomplete and/or incorrect. The latter is not hard to imagine, given the famously poor quality of doctors' handwriting.

Another problem with missing, incomplete, or incorrect medical data is related to the quality of medical research. It is very hard to come up with an effective new drug to treat a disease if there is no good underlying data to understand what is causing it. In reality, the lack of good, relevant data is the single largest obstacle in medical research. It is partially related to the difficulty, high cost, and low reliability of collecting detailed data on a large representative group of patients over long periods of time.

This is an extreme but very telling example of the value of good information. Like in war, data makes the difference between life and death.

Economics

On the economic front, the lack of data may cause political upheavals or a terminal blow to a company or industry. Poor economic data and information has led to several economic crises, with the most recent occurring in 2008.

The housing market collapse could be directly tied to the lack of information about the looming crisis in the hands of the public. However, such information existed in our collective government and bank databases. Several politicians were aware of it, but their self-interest precluded public announcements. The same can be said about the dot-com crisis as well.

In economics, like in medicine, we lack enough reliable data in general. This is related to the prohibitive cost of tracking all the detailed relevant data, as well as the impossibility of codifying human behavior and personal preferences that drive our economy. People frequently do not know their own motivation for purchasing certain items, because buying is not always rational. Even if they did know, it does not mean that they would share this personal information with researchers. For that reason, among others, we will never have perfect economic and marketing data.

Nevertheless, there is a lot of room for improvement with respect to sharing and interpreting the data and information we already collect.

One of the major drivers of company performance is the quality and integrity of top management. This is information like any other. However, this information is not readily available to stockholders because it's hard to collect, codify, and store. One of the reasons for Warren Buffett's stock-picking success is that he can personally assess that key information during dinner with a CEO—an option that is not available to small investors.

News

What is the value of news? There are two perspectives: how much we spend on it and how much it impacts our civics and governing.

As far as the monetary value, let's use $2 per day per household in the U.S. This is how much we used to spend daily on newspapers and magazines before free online versions displaced that business model. There are over 100 million households in the U.S., making it a roughly $200 million per day or $70 billion a year industry.

However, this is nothing compared to the cost of making a wrong decision on a wrong policy proposed by a wrong political candidate based on the wrong data or information published by the media.

The media, in this case, are supposed to provide data and information. You, as a reader, are supposed to turn it into your own knowledge and take a wise action by voting for the right candidate or supporting the right cause by volunteering or donating money.

The problem starts when media do not provide the right data and information while acting in the 'knowledge and wisdom' business. This fits the definition of propaganda, or the propagation of misleading information to promote or defend a particular political cause or point of view. We call it the publisher's slant, and readers ignore it at their own risk.

All oppressive regimes have used or are using propaganda as a basic tool to control populations. The two masters of this so-called craft were Joseph Goebbels, Minister of Propaganda for Hitler and the team of Pravda journalists supported by the KGB Disinformation Desk on behalf of the equally murderous communist Soviet regime.

Many non-democratic systems restrict the use of Internet and social media, and ban independent TV and radio in order to control the populace by withholding information and misleading them. A free press and totalitarianism have always been mutually exclusive.

Thus, the value of a free, unbiased press can mean the difference between freedom and life in a concentration camp or gulag.

Fraud

Most fraud is based on the misuse of data and information.

Blackmail leverages information about a victim's shameful behavior to extract money or favors. Spying and treason are selling or sharing information that compromises the defenses of a country. Insider trading is very similar to spying; in this case benefiting from information you are not supposed to have before other investors do. Destroying records is designed to hide information that may reveal nefarious activities. Hacking is getting access to information that may have commercial value and resides on a remote computer. Breach of confidentiality is sharing information that may impact the competitiveness of an enterprise.

Please note that the penalties for the above crimes of information abuse range from death to long prison sentences, and/or stiff financial penalties. Just ask the Rosenbergs or Martha Stewart.

Thus, our penal code has very harsh treatments for the misuse of information. Indirectly, the stiffness of the punishment reflects the great value of the misused information to society as a whole.

Opportunity Cost

What is the cost of not knowing or learning too late? There are several instances worth mentioning:

- A wrong policy is implemented based on wrong information. The Great Depression of 1929 is a perfect example.

- A wrong action is taken due to the lack of information. An example is increasing the price without knowing that a comparable product has been introduced by the competition.

- Increase in taxation to spur economic growth. This is a typical reaction of politicians based on the wrong information in the hands of their constituents. Never in the history of economics has higher taxes led to increased productivity. Yet, we keep trying...

- Collapse of the whole system. The communist Soviet Union collapsed due to very poor internal information of their own production reporting, among other things. The system was so corrupt as to encourage the falsification of production data by padding the real numbers. Thus, the aggregated national numbers were grossly overstated. This wrong information led to too much spending on military based on assumed national affluence. It bankrupted the whole country and led to its partitioning.

- 9/11 terrorist attack on New York and Washington D.C. The FBI had a separate database from the CIA. The FBI and CIA each knew something about some of the terrorists, but not all of their associations. The two agencies never connected the information dots.

- Losing business. Kmart has a lot of information system problems, including the lack of coordination between sales and advertising. They would post price discounts in the local newspaper, but the prices were not honored at the check-out as stores failed to adjust the prices in their database accordingly. This turned off many customers who drove directly to Walmart who matched Kmart's advertised sale prices and also had the right information at the check-out counter.

- Wrong major of study selected. As a function of a lack of information, a student selects the wrong major, goes into debt, and cannot find a job after graduation.

- On the positive side: Capitoline geese made a warning noise, providing Romans with enough timely information to avoid Gaul's invasion.

- Marathon battle after which the Greek soldier Pheidippides ran 42 kilometers to report the victory, which prevented the evacuation of Athens.

- Waze or radio reports immediately on a road closure due to an accident. A quick detour is suggested to avoid long hours sitting on a highway.

Trust

What is the price of the right information, in addition to all the benefits we discussed above?

The single largest benefit of the right information is trust. Trust in professionalism of a person providing the right and timely information.

An increase in trust decreases the cost of doing business. Without trust, we spend a lot of energy, time, and money to verify the trustworthiness of our business partners. This includes lawyers, forensic accountants, private investigators, bribes, and our own time and energy worrying about being double crossed instead of building more value. We will be discussing the impact of blockchain technologies on trust in business in later chapters.

In general, the less trust in the system, the poorer the country. Just check out Cuba, North Korea, and Venezuela.

The following three quotes provide a great perspective on trust in business:

"If people like you, they'll listen to you; but if they trust you, they'll do business with you." (Zig Ziglar)

"You may be deceived if you trust too much, but you will live in torment if you don't trust enough." (Frank Crane)

"You can fool all the people some of the time, and some of the people all the time; but you can't fool all the people all the time." (Abraham Lincoln)

Communication Gap

One of the modern barriers to utilizing the right information is the weakness in human communications. As humans we may not know, or remember, or forget to pass along information, or all of the above.

We may have access to the right data at the right time, but we may not be the right person to solve the problem. In other words, the right data may exist, but for several reasons it may not be in the right hands at the right time.

Let me give you an example: A call center rep gets the call that there is a problem with an item that has just been purchased. The call center agent queries the customer, finds the right information, and puts it in the computer. However, the salesperson does not know about the call or the problem because there is no automatic notification of such communication between a customer and the call center. The sales rep may learn about it in a few days, but it may be too late to save that account. So, the right info was in the system but....

This is a very typical scenario where a business process involves multiple professionals separated by time and location (which today is true in almost all businesses). Unless there is a workflow system with the right automatic notifications to relevant players, the ball gets dropped.

In reality, a lot of information is lost or missed between emails, voicemails, and incomplete Customer Relationship Management (CRM) systems. The person who sent the message has no way of knowing if the intended recipient got it. Even if they did know that they got it, they may not know if they did anything about it. The more individuals involved in servicing and sales, the more likely there will be gaps in communication.

The same phenomenon is experienced by large design/implementation teams. Many individuals complete separate but interdependent tasks, but it is very hard to know the status of the overall project without extensive time spent on manual tracking (which is time consuming, error prone, and distracts from actual work and creativity).

Not surprisingly, the answer to this problem came out of Silicon Valley. It was based on the need to exchange a lot of information with a lot of individuals on many concurrent worldwide software development projects in a variety of formats (text, video, images, audio) with simultaneous reporting on progress.

Thus, Slack was born—a multi-channel, multi-platform (smartphone, tablet, desktop), multi-format communication application software conceptually similar to (but far more powerful than) Facebook Messenger. You can share whatever content you want with any group you define via text interface (attaching files is supported) and all the communication is time-stamped automatically.

The right people are notified that the communication happened. You can then set up automatic updates to the overarching project management system.

The importance of this development has tremendous ramifications for the future productivity of knowledge workers. It is easy to share, update, and know if your action resulted in the corresponding related task. If not, the right party is automatically notified.

This enhances communication to a very significant degree. It increases accountability and transparency, allows for tracking progress in real time, and can be audited in the future (because every communication is time-stamped with a user-ID and tied to a task). On the minus side, it will be almost impossible to slack off anymore (no pun intended), because every action is tracked automatically.

The great success of Slack brought about competition from Microsoft, who introduced a similar product called Teams. Given the wide footprint of Microsoft in most businesses worldwide, we expect strong competition for Slack.

This type of communication/collaboration software will become a reality in the rest of the business world. It's hard to tell when, but there are too many compelling reasons for this trend not to materialize soon. Today, we waste a very large percentage of our professional time on gaps in communication.

There is no point in having better information if one cannot share it and use it in the creation of additional value. I expect Slack-type functionality to be in the business mainstream in five years, and as ubiquitous as Excel and Word are today in ten to fifteen years.

Summary

The value of data and information is hard to overestimate. It is the basis of all human activities in business, the arts, education, politics, and civics. Society cannot function well with a lack of reliable information on recent events, actual production, and consumption.

As we demonstrated, most of our wealth is related to processing data and information while blending it with knowledge and then taking the appropriate action. Good data and information is *sine qua non*, or an essential condition, to a modern, affluent, and well-governed society or enterprise.

It is then not surprising that those who do not share these values would work to restrict access to the right information, whether it's the current news or economic, business, or government statistics.

The great potential ahead for all humanity exists in the provision of a quality education so that citizens:
- Know and have access to the right information (this is in the domain of defining robust curricula in our schools)

- Have enough critical thinking skills to interpret the information and turn it into knowledge
- Can freely act, vote and/or support the effective and productive steps required for economic development based on the above.

In a practical business context, this means better and faster data collection, more knowledge about business processes, and better analytical and communication skills for more effective decision-making. One way or another, data and information are the non-negotiable components of any major future progress in business and society. Having the right data and information does not assure it, but not having it results in unfulfilled potential or even failure and social upheaval.

The latest communication/collaboration tools such as Slack and Teams will greatly help in making use of data and information in business even more effective. Today, we waste too much time on communication gaps, thus undermining the value of good information.

5

Technical Concepts

Complex Made Simple

In this section, we will go over basic digital terminology. Terminology associated with the digital revolution can be quite confusing. There are several reasons for that.

One reason is that technology vendors create marketing terms in an attempt to brand their new products and services. Given their large promotional budgets, they coin certain creative terms such as 'cloud computing'. The term becomes a popular marketing name, but means different things to different people and confuses them.

The other reason is an attempt to describe old concepts using new terms to underscore the growing importance of existing technology. Twenty years, ago we had EIS (Executive Information Systems), then DSS (Decision Support Systems), followed by OLAP (Online Analytical Processing), Data Mining, and finally, today, BI (Business

Intelligence) systems. However, over all these years, they've all been doing exactly the same thing; i.e., analyzing data and creating managerial charts and reports.

Data scientist versus old fashioned 'statistician' or 'data analyst' is another good example. Data scientist just sounds more 'cool' but the job responsibilities of analyzing data have been the same for the last century...

Yet, another example is Big Data, denoting just.... more data.

Let me explain all of these concepts in plain English, stripped of marketing spin. We will decipher:

- Big Data:
- Data Warehouse
- Analytics
- SQL
- API
- Blockchain
- Business Intelligence
- Artificial Intelligence
- Machine Learning
  ... among others.

Big Data and Data Warehouse

Big Data denotes just…. more data.

The popular term *Big Data* was coined by META Group (now Gartner, an IT research company) to describe data sets that have:

1. High volume
2. High velocity
3. High variety

High volume means a lot of data in relation to what we used to have in the past (but META Group did not define how much data makes it 'big'); high velocity, which means high speed or real time data inputs and outputs; and variety, which refers to the range of data types (unstructured text and numerics from emails, posts, images, video, and audio). Facebook data on 1.7 billion users would surely fit that definition.

Big Data is just a marketing term used to draw attention to the issues associated with the technical challenges related to the management of very large data sets that are quickly updated and contain various types of unstructured data.

In the not so distant past, most of the data to be analyzed was structured in rows and columns (think Excel) and did not change in real time (it was updated daily, weekly, or monthly). One exception is the high-speed transaction processing used by banks and large financial institutions; but even this doesn't meet the variety test.

Today, data also comes from emails, posts, comments, images, videos, and audio files, and it keeps changing non-stop in real time.

- Definition of 'Big' by Meta Group
  - High volume
  - High velocity - lots of updates in real time
  - High variety - text, image, video, audio
- Marketing term
- Drawing attention to challenges of managing very large databases
- In the past, most data was just numbers in neat rows and columns

Today's data, whether big or small, is the foundation of all business transactions and the *de facto* business currency. It is the digital glue in digital disruption, the digitization of existing processes, and the creation of new products and services. All these activities require a lot of data to work well. They also generate lots of data.

- New business currency
- Digital glue in the digital revolution, which ...needs a lot of data and...
- ...generates a lot of data

The best examples are social media platforms that are both data hungry and data intensive. Their success is based on the ability to collect as much relevant data as they can so they can sell it to advertisers. Their value is directly proportional to the number of users and their activities—hence data. Imagine the technical complexity of managing Facebook data generated by more than 1.7 billion users, constantly creating and sharing enormous amounts of new content globally.

Another example is an e-commerce site. To build an e-commerce site, we need product data, communication data, security data, and room to store all future transaction data. Next we need customer data to design and implement a marketing campaign. Then we start collecting all the web traffic data, data on the behaviors of visitors and prospects on our website before they decided to buy, and then transaction data after the actual sale. Finally, we need fulfillment data, shipment data, and returns data, to name a few. Imagine the amount of data behind Amazon's e-commerce site, which sells 480 thousands different products.

Internet of Things applications tend to create a lot of data as well. Imagine thousands of sensors residing on an oil platform sending measurement results to a central processor every millisecond.

- Social media
- E-commerce
- The Internet of Things

From the analytical perspective, the amount of data may be irrelevant to the process of discovering patterns in the data. Actually, a lot of valid research can be done on a good sample of data. We do not always need all of the data to draw statistically valid conclusions. Also, more data does not necessarily mean better data—especially if it is incorrect, irrelevant, or incomplete.

However, we need all data when we want to summarize all transactions or do detailed reports broken down by various categories such as product, region, customer, etc.

- Bigger does not mean better
- Can do research on sample data
- Need all data for summaries and management reports

Data Warehouse, Data Mart, Data Lake

Data Warehouse is a term used to denote the functional scope and physical space where certain business data is stored. A Data Warehouse usually stores data belonging to a particular business department. Data Warehouse is just a marketing term applied to large business databases.

Conceptually, Big Data may reside in a Data Warehouse.

Companies would have a Sales Data Warehouse, a Financial Data Warehouse, or a Marketing Data Warehouse (or Mart or Lake) denoting the scope of their logical functionality.

'Marts' and 'Lakes' usually denote smaller databases, or logical subsets of larger entities. Thus, the Marketing Data Warehouse can be made up of a Social Media Data Mart (or Lake) and a Web Traffic Data Mart (or Lake).

If vendors continue along these lines of naming conventions, we may soon have Data Pools, Data Ponds, and Data Puddles.

From the technical and analytical perspective, these terms are completely irrelevant. Data analysis always included queries against databases, regardless of how they are named, how they related to each other, or how big they were.

- Databases organized by business function
  o Sales Data Warehouse
  o Marketing Data Warehouse
  o Financial Data Warehouse

- Marketing Data Warehouse may be made up of
  o Social Media Data Mart
  o Web Traffic Data Mart
  o Online Advertising Data Mart

- From a technical and analytical perspective, they are all just databases

SQL - Structured Query Language

Almost all business data today is stored in relational databases. Imagine a database made up of multiple Excel sheets (they are actually called 'tables'). There is one sheet for all customers, one

GREG GUTKOWSKI

sheet for all products, and one sheet for all
salespeople. Like in Excel, you have different
columns for different sheets.

What is relevant to customers may not be relevant
to products. For example, products will not have a
physical address and customers will not have a
color. So it does not make sense to create one big
sheet with columns mixing characteristics of
products and customers. Yet, for analysis purposes
we may want to combine them.

Rather than combining them in one sheet or table,
we combine them by writing reports using
Standard Query Language. Like any other
computer language, it has its own syntax and rules.
A simple SQL code phrase may look like this:

Select 'Customer Name' from 'Customer_Table'
Where Product = 'iPad'

As you can guess, this request will print out all
customers stored in a table called 'Customer_Table'
who purchased iPads.

However, before the computer can execute such a
request, we need to combine two sheets; one with
customer data and one with product data. The
product table will have one row for each sale
storing who bought what. In other words, it will
have the customer ID number associated with each
item purchased. The same unique number will be
used in 'Customer_Table'. As you would expect, we
will use customer ID number to combine, or 'join',

two tables or sheets to put them on the same line in the report.

So think of SQL as a utility that allows us to join or combine various sheets by using unique ID numbers. After we join them, we can then create reports with information from multiple tables.

In most business data warehouses, the number of separate tables or sheets will exceed a hundred; sometimes a complex query needs to be constructed to go across the spectrum of business activities. Imagine analyzing social media, email, paid advertising, web traffic, sales, customer service, and profitability stored in eight separate tables. You would need to join all eight sources of data before writing reports against it.

For an excellent overview of SQL, you may want to watch this YouTube video:

https://www.youtube.com/watch?v=7Vtl2WggqO g

Application Programming Interface (API)

Yes, we store a lot of business data in internal database tables. However, when we want to combine information from two different websites using just browsers, SQL is of no help in making that connection.

For example, when you have a weather app on your smartphone, your iPhone or Galaxy does not store all the weather data on it—it just stores your location. When you want to check out the local weather for today, you click on a button to open a weather app. Behind the scenes, the app picks up your location and today's date. Then your smartphone sends your location and today's date to the central cloud-based database where all the weather data is stored for all days and all cities.

At the same time, the app passes the request to return only the data for your particular city and just for today. Based on that request, the central database returns a small file with the info on the weather for your city today. After it reaches your smartphone, it gets formatted nicely to fit your screen, and *voila!*—in a few seconds you have info on the rainfall or sunshine coming soon to your town.

What has just been described above is accomplished using an Application Programming Interface or API. It's a technical term for a way to exchange data between various software applications on the Internet today, including 'handshakes' between requests coming from browsers or smartphone apps.

All the software developers who work with apps and other Internet applications have already agreed to a standard API method of passing information back and forth between smartphones or browsers and the central databases. Just like we all agreed to drive on the right side of the road and have the gas and brake pedals in our cars next to each other with the accelerator being on the right side. To use another analogy, such a standard is equivalent to agreeing to speak the same language, thus avoiding the complexity of knowing many and having to translate from one to another.

Another useful analogy is to think about an API in terms of eating out at a local restaurant. As a restaurant customer, you and your party give your orders to the waiter, who accepts the order and in turn passes the request to the kitchen, which, after some time, returns the dish you ordered via a waiter. In any restaurant, there are many parties and customers, many waiters, many menu items, and one kitchen. They all speak English (or a local language) and hopefully you and your party are served what you actually ordered in the desired amount of time and at the right temperature. The waiter is your API.

In a nutshell, this is all you need to know about APIs if you are not a programmer. One thing to keep in mind as a non-programmer, is that any application your business develops may also benefit from accepting data requests via API. A good example here is providing managerial reports to your customers on the status of services you provide.

Imagine you manage a large apartment complex and you have all the data on all the requests for repairs from all the tenants stored together with the status of repairs. You built that database to coordinate all repair jobs. You can also provide tenants with a web page or phone app where they can check on the status of just their requests.

A question to ask when evaluating any commercial software today is whether it supports exchanging data via API. If they do not, look elsewhere.

Blockchain

'Trust but verify' - Russian proverb

Imagine that every online transaction ever done by anyone, anytime, is going to be stored in a secure database forever, tagged with a timestamp and the name of the person who entered it online. No one can hack it, no one can edit it, and no one can delete it. It is one hundred percent secure, forever, and easy to verify by anyone who was involved in it, because each transaction can be easily looked up at anytime. No dictator or government agency can ever change it, and no drug or oil money can corrupt it.

For a moment, let's not worry about the technology involved. Let me just assure you that this is technically feasible today and already being used around the world on a limited basis.

By 'transaction' I mean popular online activities such as:

- Paying a bill online
- Receiving a single invoice payment

- Sending or receiving money transfers to or from a family member

- Signing online contracts with e-signature
- Uploading a document
- Editing a contract
- Sending or receiving email

- Shipping a product
- Receiving a product

- Voting
- Responding to a survey
- Filling out a form requesting information
- Applying for jobs, permits, or memberships

- Downloading a song or a picture
- Clicking on an advertisement
- Viewing a video or a streamed movie

- Updating your health records by your doctor
- Filling prescriptions

Let's talk about the implications. The single largest one is enhanced TRUST based on TRANSPARENCY.

Do you really trust your bank one hundred percent to not ever make a mistake transferring your money? Do you trust your bank to be one hundred percent hack-proof and that your identity will never be stolen? Few do.

Do you really trust that your documents (deeds, wills, contracts, agreements) will never be stolen, destroyed, or changed without your knowledge by omission or commission? Or your signature forged? Few do.

Do your really know where the products you buy came from, and what they're really made of, and what health inspections they were subject to? Few do.

Do you really trust that all of our municipal, state, and federal votes or opinion polls were correctly and truthfully tabulated? Few do.

Do you think that artists today have a good idea who has sold their songs, movies, or images in what quantities and how much royalties they should really receive? Few do.

Do you think that advertisers today really trust Google and Facebook with respect to the actual number of times an ad was displayed and clicked on? Few do.

Do you think that Google and Facebook have your privacy interests in mind? Few do.

Do you think that your medical records are safe in terms of privacy? Few do.

Do you think that your prescription drug purchase records are safe from hacking? Few do.

Do you think that tax agencies (federal and state) can trust the integrity of your tax returns? Do you think taxpayers trust federal and state tax agencies with respect to the right amount of taxes owed? Few do (because the rules are too numerous, hard to understand and follow in most countries in the world).

Now imagine that in all the scenarios described above, all the involved parties can trust each other because they can easily verify every transaction with a few clicks.

The implications are **ENORMOUS,** with many more that are hard to imagine today.

If we were to implement blockchain technology across the board, the following things would happen:

- The majority of banks, tax auditors, tax preparers, and tax attorneys, would cease to exist. So would federal, state, and municipal tax agencies. This would help reduce budget deficits and result in an overall reduction in government expenditures, which could and should be passed on to voters in the form of lower taxes. It would also result in a significant reduction in financial and legal fees that are passed on to customers.

- Elimination of money laundering and severe reduction in systemic corruption. Fewer politicians will be tempted to abuse power. It would be almost impossible to hide illicit supplemental income.

- Severe reduction in the number of lawyers defending contracts and litigating contract breaches. There would be no need for so many of them because it would be very hard to breach a contract in the first place. The savings on lawyer fees would be passed on to customers.

- Less fraud and thus the need for fewer lawyers, judges, prosecutors, and jail facilities. It would be much harder to defraud in the first place. The savings would be passed on to taxpayers and consumers.

- Increase in the quality and healthfulness of our food, with a simultaneous decrease in the price of food because it would be easy to identify and eliminate dishonest suppliers and/or low-quality ingredients.

- More trust in civics because voting fraud would be completely eliminated. More trust in the media because poll reliability would increase. More voter engagement will follow as a result of less cynicism associated with the lack of governing transparency and less corruption.

- More effective advertising. Savings passed on to consumers—not Google.

- Better health records leading to better research and thus better outcomes. Potentially huge savings throughout society.

- More creative artists less frustrated with being ripped off, and more inspiration for our souls.

In a nutshell, it is hard to overestimate the impact of more trust. One thing is certain: the use of technology enforces more accountability and transparency. This translates to trust. Trust translates to a lower cost of doing business, more social cohesion, more citizen participation, more creative expression, and more productivity because rewards are more justly tied to outcomes. Isn't it what we are all really striving for?

I've presented here only a few tangible but tremendous benefits derived from recording, keeping, and protecting every online transaction and the trust that results. There are many more that we may not be able to envision today. Just like it was hard for anyone to envision a portable camera combined with a portable phone (today called a smartphone) when Graham Bell first presented his phone in 1876, almost forty years before the first 35mm camera was introduced in 1913.

A fundamental change like this is not going to happen overnight because too many forces today have too much to lose from it. However, this is an inescapable trend, loaded with a lot of great and optimistic possibilities. The question is not whether it will happen. It is already happening. The question is when it will happen on a large, worldwide scale.

For your reference, here is Wikipedia's technical definition of blockchain as a technology.

A **blockchain**—originally **block chain**—is a continuously growing list of records, called blocks, which are linked and secured using cryptography. Each block typically contains a hash pointer as a link to a previous block, a timestamp, and transaction data. By design, blockchains are inherently resistant to modification of the data. Harvard Business Review defines it as "an open, distributed ledger that can record transactions between two parties efficiently and in a verifiable and permanent way." For use as a distributed ledger, a blockchain is typically managed by a peer-to-peer network collectively adhering to a protocol for validating new blocks. Once recorded, the data in any given block cannot be altered retroactively without the alteration of all subsequent blocks, which would require collusion in the majority of the network.

Business Intelligence (BI) Software

It's very time consuming to write SQL statements to analyze data. There are several software vendors who provide tools where SQL code is being generated behind the scenes and a user can create reports by clicking, dragging and dropping, or selecting parameters from drop-down boxes.

In 2018, the global annual market for such tools is about $10 billion in sales.

Despite their marketing claims, they all perform over ninety percent of the same actions. Just like Excel compared to Google Sheets. They vary in pricing, some graphical niceties, and ease of use, but anyone can do good business analysis with all of them.

There are several reliable software 'players', shown here in no particular order. The differences between them are like those between a Honda Accord and a Toyota Camry. Today, the acronym used for business analytics software is 'BI', or Business Intelligence.

- SAS
- Tableau
- Information Builders
- Micro-strategy
- Domo
- Power BI from Microsoft

For a full, current, and ever-changing list, please refer to Gartner Magic Quadrant for Business Intelligence and Analytics Platforms. Gartner offers an annual service evaluating each vendor in depth. Like with most digital technologies a lot of hyped vendors come and go, and a lot of reliable players have been on their list for over twenty years.

In my experience, BI tools are seldom the bottleneck in business analysis. With the right training, they are not very hard to use. What *is hard* is getting good quality data and understanding non-measurable business context to come up with the right analysis.

Many companies overestimate the importance of BI tools in the whole analytical process. Usually, they are the easiest to implement and manage compared to the complexity of managing the integrity and relevance of business data stored in data warehouses

Artificial Intelligence (AI) and Machine Learning (ML)

Speaking of Artificial Intelligence and Machine Learning... We consider them to be just marketing terms. From the analytical perspective, they are just very sophisticated software algorithms used against a variety of either very complex and/or voluminous data.

These algorithms require a lot of computing power or a lot of algorithmic logic, or both, to accomplish the task of optimizing a process. Algorithms are written by humans based on their business knowledge combined with their experience in

computer science, and mathematics, statistics, psychology, linguistics, and neuroscience.
Is speech recognition an example of artificial intelligence? We think not. It's just an optimal way to recognize speech.

Several years ago, optical character recognition (OCR), or turning scanned text into data, was considered AI, until it became a boring but very productive routine.

At the end of the day, at the processing level, all data is just a bunch of 0s and 1s, whether it's photos, video, audio, text, or numbers, or a combination of these. There is no artificial intelligence or machine learning. The intelligence and learning are in the development and implementation of algorithms that can take advantage of the available data and existing computer power.

"Computers are incredibly fast, accurate but stupid; humans are incredibly slow, inaccurate but brilliant; together they are powerful beyond imagination."
Unknown

This quote is a perfect summarization of the contribution of humans and machines to so-called artificial intelligence, machine learning, and the digital revolution in general.

There has been a lot of talk recently about the dangers of self-aware AI robots replacing our jobs, killing innocent souls, ruining our planet, and finishing off our civilization.

I'm skeptical about this fear-mongering by the media because AI is nothing but mathematical algorithms processing a bunch of 0s and 1s, and as such is incapable of ever thinking, reasoning, or threatening anyone.

As discussed before, AI and Machine Learning are just technical marketing terms used to sell more software, hardware, services, and research around mathematical algorithms that have been around for years. The only new things are increased computing power and more data to feed it. More power seldom makes things more intelligent.

More data may help, but that data needs to be relevant, timely, correct, and granular enough to make the whole concept work. The problem is that we lack the right data to explain most of the problems we are trying to solve today (despite collecting tons of data in general).

In meteorology, we can't even predict the weather in our towns in the next twelve hours so we are confident we can leave our umbrellas behind. Why not? Because we do not have enough granular atmospheric data for our weather-prediction models. Collecting relevant weather data is prohibitively expensive, so our weather stations are sparsely located.

In medical research, we do not have enough granular, longitudinal, reliable, consistent, and clean data to learn what causes our bodies to stop producing insulin, or what causes most cancers or even the common flu. We don't even have a consistent medical patient records database to manage basic healthcare needs!

In business, ninety-nine percent of companies keep data in silos (for marketing, sales, customer service, and finance) that don't talk to each other, which prevents us from the basic discovery of what really drives profits. Thus, a lot of resources are wasted on guesstimates. Case in point: it is almost impossible to attribute actual sales to most social media posts (not ads). The same is true with most radio, TV, and print advertising.

In economics, despite there being tons of data collected by the government and Wall Street, one can hardly spot down-cycles and warn the public about them. Remember the dot.com and 2008 crashes?

In politics, during the last U.S. elections, the media told us that one candidate had a more than ninety-five percent chance of winning just a few days before we learned otherwise. It was not a lack of computing power that led to such a mistaken conclusion.

We do well with algorithms when the data is clean, relevant, and plentiful. For example, computers can identify a malignant tumor from a high-resolution scan, but only because there are enough relevant pixels in the picture (computers are fed thousands of pictures of affected and healthy patient data so they can 'learn' from comparing the two sets). Yet, the same computer does not know what caused this tumor or how to cure it....because it lacks appropriate data in the first place.

In a nutshell, we do not have the relevant data (granular, timely, and correct) to solve the majority of problems faced by humanity today, including healthcare, economics, weather, marketing, and politics.

Thus, the Achilles heel of AI and Machine Learning hype is the lack of the right data. Despite lots of computing power, sophisticated data models and analytical software. It's like driving a Tesla with no suspension.

- Require powerful algorithms
- May require a lot of computing power
- Written by humans
- Just another optimization process
- Intelligence is in writing and implementing algorithms

Summary

This chapter introduced the basic technical concepts that are integral parts of the measurement revolution. Without understanding these technologies, one runs the risk of making less than optimal decisions when planning the technological infrastructure, organizational change, and training needed to take full advantage of them.

The following military analogy is very helpful here. When the military was moving away from horses and swords and turning to helicopters and Tomahawk missiles, they had to understand the impact of these new technologies on the military strategy, organization of units, and relevant training.

As one is not expected to feed hay to a helicopter, one should not be expected to skip the training necessary to achieve readiness up to par with new technologies.

- Big Data
- Data Warehouse
- Analytics
- SQL
- API
- Blockchain
- Business Intelligence
- Artificial Intelligence
- Machine Learning

6

Key Performance Indicators
'From Tweet to Profit'

Now that we've discussed the value of information and the key technologies to manage it, it's time to explore how to measure company business performance.

KPIs or Key Performance Indicators are quantifiable measures used to gauge progress toward established goals. It's a common business term adopted by the majority of publicly-owned companies today.

KPIs are sets of measures used to determine strategic and operational goals for a company. After all, strategic results are a function of good operational execution. In addition, KPIs can be used to compare a company to industry standards or regional performance.

For example, every business has explicit or implicit sales goals or expectations for annual sales. Therefore, the expected annual goal for sales would be a very popular KPI in any industry and any size business.

KPIs are usually presented as actual achievement versus the planned one. They come with the corresponding difference (variance) shown in absolute numbers as well as percentages. Here is a typical example of a sales KPI:

KPI	Actual	Goal	Variance in $	Variance in %
Sales	$ 120,000	$ 100,000	$ 20,000	20%

The company planned to sell $100,000 worth of products in a given period, but it exceeded the goal by $20,000 or twenty percent.

The table above allows managers to very quickly assess performance improvement or lack thereof. The actual and percentage variances appearing next to each other help them understand if a large jump in sales in terms of percentage also means a lot of revenue. If a company has many products, some may increase in sales a lot in terms of percentages, but they may account for very little revenue. The ideal situation is where both numbers are very high.

As you can imagine, one KPI is not enough to assess company performance. High sales growth may not translate into profitability—we may be giving the business away. High sales and growing sales do not necessarily mean increased market share—your competition may be growing even faster.

The ultimate KPI is the value of the company. For public companies, it's the stock price (or total value of outstanding shares). For privately-owned companies, it's an independent valuation. In most industries and for most companies, the ultimate goal is to create as much value for shareholders as possible.

Flying By The Seat Of Your Pants Versus Flying By Wire

In the early days of aviation, there were very few instruments on board to guide flight. A pilot used his own best judgment because he had few instruments and no radio. One input was the feeling of the pressure on their pants associated with ascending, descending, acceleration, and/or and sharp turns.

This technique would not work very well on today's jets. All modern aircraft are flown by wire. This means that the pilot makes most decisions by reading the instruments and not by relying on his trousers. In addition, a lot of instruments are interconnected and ultimately allow for automatic piloting at cruising altitudes.

This is a great analogy for KPIs today. In the past, a lot of businesses were built and run by the seat of the owners' pants. Instrumentation, data, and information were substituted with guessing, experience, and gut feelings.

This is, however, impractical today, given the complexity of modern enterprises. With the decreasing cost of measurement (as discussed earlier) we can provide managers with much more reliable measures of performance.

Think of KPIs as running a business by wire. You are in the business cockpit, which is full of well-designed instruments showing historical and real time data and information leading to a safe landing associated with high shareholder value.

Just like the design of instruments in a jet cockpit is the job of the top aircraft engineer, the job of top managers is to decide what gauges your business cockpit contains. With the wrong design, you may be flying in circles and crash financially. With the right KPI design, you may fly high, safe, and profitable.

Easier Said Than Done

Designing a KPI cockpit is not a trivial matter for many reasons:

1. Usually, management and shareholders agree that the number one KPI is company value, profits, or revenues. However, they may not agree on what these numbers should or could be. For example, do we want to grow five percent or fifty percent?

2. Even if they agree on a desired growth rate, there are many different ways to achieve the goals. For example, increase prices or

introduce new products, but only in a few regions or countries?

3. Even if they agree on how to achieve these goals, they may not agree on how to measure them. For example, how would we know that our production is going to materialize if the new product design and testing takes twelve months?

Where the jet cockpit analogy falls short is that, in business, the main cockpit results are made up of the result of the underlying units that can be geographically dispersed and run by less senior managers. This is not the case on a jetfighter where a single pilot has total, direct control over the overall performance of the flight.

Thus, each of the subordinate managers or business functions needs to have its own cockpit. This will be true for marketing, sales, finance, operations, customer service, etc. Now, the problems associated with the design of a perfect ultimate cockpit are multiplied by the number of units and sub-units.

In larger corporations, internal competition between key managers could cause problems securing the necessary cooperation between business units.

Thus, as great as the concept of KPIs is, they have three major limitations:

1. Do not reflect the real goals of a unit (lack of knowledge or internal politics or both)

2. Do not reflect the aligned goals necessary for corporate success (internal competition between units)

3. Do not have enough relevant and good data to support real goal measurement

Nevertheless, even with the limitations, employing KPIs is the single best way to measure and communicate company performance, both internally and to shareholders. It's the job of top managers to address the three limitations described above. After all, if everything was perfect already, we would not need so many managers and business students.

Business cockpits with KPIs are frequently referred to as 'managerial dashboards' or just 'dashboards'. We will be discussing them in more depth in a subsequent chapter devoted to visualization and business storytelling.

KPI Categories

Each publicly owned company and a lot of privately owned ones across all industries have KPIs grouped in basic categories. The most popular categories are:

1. Overall Corporate - Revenue, Profit, Valuation
2. Marketing - Market Share, Customer Satisfaction, Customer Engagement
3. Sales - Units Sold By Product and/or Division/State/Country

4. Financial - Return on Investment, Debt, Payables, Receivables
5. Human Resources - Number of Employees, Employee Cost, Retention

Depending on the industry, they may have a set of specific KPIs:

1. Logistics and Transportation
2. Manufacturing
3. Health Care
4. Education
5. Sports

Quantitative vs. Qualitative

A quantitative KPI is a measure based on numbers that can be easily added, subtracted, multiplied, or divided and still make business sense. Thus, the following examples meet these criteria:

1. Revenues
2. Profits
3. Number of Customers
4. Costs
5. Number of widgets produced

You can add revenues for all states to come up with the total country revenues, for example. You can divide revenue by cost to calculate margin. You can calculate profit per widget. Most KPIs used in business are quantitative.

A qualitative KPI is usually based on opinions (usually those of customers, but they could also come from employees through a workplace satisfaction survey). The most important and most popular is a customer satisfaction measure called Net Promoter Value. It measures how customers ranked your company on a ten-point satisfaction scale. A similar phenomenon is associated with five-star ratings on social media platforms such as Yelp or Google. Another example is customer preferences for product features.

Leading Versus Lagging

A leading KPI reflects the initial result of a bigger process that has not yet been completed. The best example is the number of visits to a website as a result of a marketing campaign. Having a lot of visitors is a leading indicator of success, but does not guarantee it.

The actual results in sales or profit would be conclusive proof of a campaign's success. Thus, the lagging indicator is one that reflects the total result of a long, multi-step process.

Leading indicators

1. Emails opened
2. Website visits
3. Parts received

Lagging indicators

1. Widgets produced
2. Products sold
3. Profits earned

The difference between leading and lagging is arbitrary. The idea is to measure the early success of a long, multi-step process. The longer the process and the more steps it has, the more value there is in measuring intermediate steps.

This is especially true in digital marketing campaigns where there are many distinct, consecutive steps (social media posts, emails, visits to the web, form filling, request for price, actual purchase, returns, etc.). Closely watching each step may alert us to a process breakdown.

For example, people may visit your website, but they are abandoning your shopping cart a lot. You may want to know this as quickly as possible without waiting for the bad news weeks from now.

Descriptive Versus Predictive

Descriptive KPIs depict what really happened. They are factual and not disputable (assuming the data is correct). These include actual sales, profits, costs, shipments, etc.

Predictive KPIs include guesses, estimations, and forecasts. The most popular of these is Sales Forecast. It is a very important measure for planning production, for example. Yet, this is just a best guess regardless of the statistical methods used.

The same is true for fraud prediction and for lending based on customer credit-scoring.

Another predictive measure forecasts possible future equipment failure in manufacturing operations.

Most KPIs are descriptive, but there is a growing importance on using data to predict outcomes before they materialize to improve planning, purchasing, and logistics.

Real Versus Sample

Real measures are involved when money is being exchanged or reported. Financial and accounting measures are perfect examples. One needs to balance the books precisely—there is no rounding up or down. The same is true when paying bills or when reporting financial results by publicly-owned companies.

We cannot always use real measures in real life. A good example is medical research or political polls. It would be financially prohibitive and impractical to include everyone involved in cancer research or opinion polls. Hence, we use samples of populations. If the right sampling methods are used, this could be a good approximation, given the alternative.

Sampling is also frequently done in manufacturing for quality control purposes.

Marketing And Sales KPIs

Since marketing and sales efforts include many distinct interlocking steps stretched, sometimes, over very long time periods (it's not unusual to have twelve-month sales cycles in business for large deals), let's examine and discuss typical KPIs along the whole process that starts with promotions and ends with… product returns (hopefully not).

Promotions

- The number of emails sent
- The number of emails opened
- The number of email clicks
- The number of impressions displayed
- The number of ads clicked on
- The number of social media posts
- Social media engagement
- Social media sentiment

Website Traffic

- The number of website visitors by channel
- New vs. returning
- Bounce rate
- The number visitors by duration of a visit
- The number of engagements
- Number of downloads
- Number of forms filled
- Number of phone calls made
- Number of chats

- Number of text messages

Salesforce KPIs

- Number of interactions
- Calls made/emails sent
- Number of appointments made
- Number of presentations made
- Number of proposals made
- Number of sales

- Number of emails sent
- Number of emails opened
- Number of emails clicked
- Number of visits to certain pages
- Number of downloads
- Number of forms filled

- Cost per email
- Cost per call
- Cost per appointment
- Cost per lead
- Downloads
- Forms filled

Sales KPIs

- Sales = Revenues
- Revenue is function of
- New Customers vs. Existing
- Share of a wallet

- Price
- Competition
- Economy

- Customer demographics
- Age, gender, income, new, existing
- Customer retention
- Customer satisfaction

- Quantity, Cost of Sales, Revenue, Returns
- By product
- By customer
- By salesperson and sales territories
- By price
- By hour, day, week, month, quarter, year, etc.

Profit and ROI

- Profit
  o By products
  o By various customer demographics
  o By territory and sales person
  o By channel

In this book, we have concentrated on marketing and sales metrics as they are relevant across all industries, countries, and business sizes. There are thousands of industry- and process-related KPIs. To discover the most popular ones, or to get inspired by what is being used by other companies in your industry, just do an Internet search by typing 'KPI for x industry' or 'KPI for a process Y'.

The trick is not to discover a non-existent one. The trick is to select the set of existing KPIs that have been used successfully by other companies that can help you grow your own business.

My Favorite KPIs

The number of KPIs can be overwhelming, especially in marketing and long B2B sales cycles.

But more does not always mean better. As humans, we all have limited attention spans and no one can make sense of hundreds of measures to be tracked at the same time.

Selecting the right KPIs and motivating employees to reach them is the number one job of top executives. KPIs have to be relevant, actionable, and easy to understand and communicate. Otherwise, they defeat the purpose and are not going to be used in real decision-making. This would be similar to having too many instruments that would distract even the most skillful airplane pilot.

In my experience working with companies of all sizes in many key industries, I've learned to like these top five universal metrics or KPIs:

1. Cost per sale
2. Profit by product
3. Cost by employee
4. Customer retention
5. Customer lifetime value

Ad 1. Watching total costs in relation to sales is probably the single best way to stop runaway spending in relation to new revenue on any level of the organization. When sales are up, managers tend to be over-optimistic and lower their sensitivity to spending.

This KPI is relatively easy to get, especially at high levels and could be analyzed weekly to quickly spot wrong or good trends. I cannot imagine running any business of any size without knowing that metric.

Ad 2. Profit per product is a great way to learn which products inhibit profitability. In companies with multiple products, this key number is not always known by product. This prevents the discovery and elimination of loss leaders. Sometimes eliminating several products can dramatically improve the bottom line.

Ad 3. Employees are most likely the single largest cost of any business. If you are spending too much on employment, your margins will suffer in relation to the competition. If you are not spending enough, you may face employee turnover and the associated high cost of hiring and training replacements. A tough tradeoff, always...

Ad 4. Customer retention is of the utmost importance because the cost of selling to an existing customer is usually five to ten times less than selling the same product to a new customer. For any company that sells multiple complementary products to the same customer, this is a 'must have' KPI.

Ad 5. Customer lifetime value, which is related to customer retention; however, it's possible to retain customers but not make money. All marketing and sales efforts should be focused on positively impacting that number.

Summary

KPIs are similar to GPS for a fleet operator. They should help you decide where your units are going, how fast, when they will arrive, and where to detour if necessary. They should also warn you about the hazards of stalled profits or market crushes.

As imperfect as KPIs may be, they are indispensable managerial measurement tools. Due to the trend toward better and cheaper measurements in general, the relevance of KPIs will only grow.

By examining the quality of a KPI system, one can very quickly assess the quality of senior managers.

Next, we will introduce the most popular and powerful ways to analyze KPIs when they show negative variance from expectations.

7

How To Analyze Business Data

Let's assume that we have successfully set up all the KPIs for an organization. Everyone has a nice dashboard with clearly defined goals.

Now, what do we do when the dashboard shows we are behind schedule, about to miss a goal, or otherwise deficient? No dashboard will provide these answers automatically anytime soon. We will have all the information in front of us; the next step would be to use our knowledge and judgment to form a hypothesis of what may be causing an unfavorable variance. Sometimes, it will just take a glance at a screen; sometimes it will take weeks and a lot of investigation into the root cause of our problem. In a nutshell, the process of business analysis has just begun....

Analysis of business data is much like good journalism. We need to tell the story by answering these five fundamental questions:

1. Who?

2. What?
3. Where?
4. When?
5. Why?

The concept of the 5 Ws is nothing new. Hermagoras of Temnos, a Greek scholar, introduced this rhetorical idea during the first century BC. Since then, it has been widely used in journalism, education, law, and criminal investigations, among others.

The answers to the first four questions need to be based solely on indisputable facts (if known). In business, an example would be: Who bought the most widgets in Florida last month? The answer to this question should be relatively easy to get based on existing reports and databases.

However, when answering 'why?', we may be faced with many different and unknown reasons. Thus, we need to formulate a hypothesis and then verify it.

This is easier said than done. For example, sales may go up or down based on a multitude of factors or their combinations:

1. New price is too high
2. Competition entered the market
3. Customer had purchased the most they could from us (how many $70K cars can a dealer sell to a single client in one year?)

4. Customer has no money. Could be a local downturn due to the weakness in the local economy, or a business customer is experiencing a downturn in their business
5. Our product was not available on shelves due to transportation problems; did not make it to the store
6. Our product was not put on shelves by our distribution partner; it made it to the store but the stocking staff did not get to it
7. Our sales manager is going through a tough divorce or some other family emergency and did not follow up with the supplier
8. Our product quality has deteriorated
9. We got an unfavorable write-up in a local newspaper or social media (regardless if factual or not)
10. We did not execute our marketing campaign very well
11. Our sales person did not follow up
12. We had problems accepting payments
13. Our website was down or very slow
14. There was bad weather, a natural disaster, or a special event
15. Our company got involved in a serious lawsuit
16. Manager A is sabotaging manager B while competing for the top executive job
17. We did not give customer support agents enough information about a new product

The list above is by no means conclusive and will vary by type of industry and product. Nevertheless, please note that there is very little information in existing corporate databases to quickly answer any of these questions. Actually, most of this information may not exist in the corporate databases at all. This will be mostly true for items 1, 2, 4, 5, 6, 7, 9, 11, 14, and 16 for sure. Thus, how do we find the answer to the most important question of 'Why'?

We do it just like any good journalist or a criminal investigator. We pick up the phone and start talking to the right people. If we suspect that they are stonewalling us, we may need to see them in person. We ask questions of more-experienced managers to limit the scope of our hypothesis. We use our own knowledge and judgment to seek out the most likely causes. We check around with all relevant parties, including customers and suppliers. It may take days or weeks before we come up with the right answer.

Then, we present the results to senior managers for their decision and action. Managers may need to take some risk. Their action may require capital, which they may not have at the moment.

This is why business analysis and decision-making will never be replaced by Artificial Intelligence. It involves too many unknowns that are codified nowhere and are thus unavailable to include in even the most sophisticated algorithms in the most powerful computers.

Ideally, businesses should be run by facts and verified hypotheses about why certain things happened. In reality, due to enormous complexity and the lack of data, most businesses are run on opinions and guesstimates, and not always supported by facts. This may explain the high failure rate among businesses, especially in the early stages of their existence.

It is easier to run an established business with some historical data to lean on as compared to a startup where there is no history to fall back on. It is also easier to run a traditional business that is not high-tech and where the underlying product or service changes are not that frequent and dramatic. Compare running a funeral home to a software or electronics hardware company.

The lack of objective data also explains why political skills are very important in running an enterprise. Not all decisions will be fact-based and we need to be able to gather support based on guesstimates, personal charisma, and overall personal credibility and experience.

By the way, to be good at analyzing business, in addition to practicing the 5 Ws, we need to exhibit the following 5 Cs:

- Curiosity
- Critical thinking
- Common sense
- Creativity
- Communication

Business analysis is an art, not a science. It's a tough discipline but a great training ground for top executive jobs, including CEO.

Science in the form of statistics helps, but it accounts for a very small percentage of skills needed to succeed in business analysis. We need to be curious, creative in finding alternatives, and able to communicate effectively. In addition, common sense and critical thinking are probably the most important characteristics of a top analytical mind. The most important skill of a top analyst is asking the right questions—not statistical wizardry.

This quote is a great summary for this section:

"I seek not to know the answers, but to understand the questions." Jörn-Steffen Pischke

Types Of Business Data

Let's switch gears and discuss an organization with existing business data. After all, this is where every analysis needs to start.

As we discussed, most sales and marketing data resides today in databases made of relational tables and is accessible via SQL. When we analyze data, we usually think of rows and columns, just like in Excel. Usually, rows of data represent individual customers, products, states, sales people, etc. Let's stay with this analogy and think about an Excel spreadsheet containing a list of customers with their corresponding purchases. Imagine we are working with apparel store data.

Thus, we have three types of data organized in columns:

1. Dimensions
2. Measures
3. Time

Dimensions would be a characteristic or demographic of a customer. So, there will be a separate column for customer age, city, state, gender, product they bought, product color, and product size, for example.

Usually, dimensions are expressed as a text field and no mathematics can be performed on it. For example, it wouldn't make sense to add two colors or two addresses to each other. But we may want to perform a count of those attributes.

Dimensions can have their own hierarchy. For example, domestic customers can be grouped into states, cities, and zip codes. Or products can be organized by product line: clothing versus shoes, by product type (for women, men, and children).

Dimensions may have attributes such as a 4th of July theme. This allows us to track products that do not belong to any hierarchies or even the same producer in one easy-to-track group. For example: flags, chairs, napkins, table covers, and greeting cards can be grouped together. That would also work for Christmas, Thanksgiving, Easter, and Valentine's Day, among others.

Dimension may have an attribute of color. For example, I may want to track all navy blue apparel and shoes because that color may be hot or not that season.

For practical reasons, here is an example of dimensions **(in bold).**

- Sales **by state**
- Sales **by city**
- Sales **by zip**
- Sales **by product**
- Shipment **by store**
- Cost **by product**
- Returns **by manufacturer**
- Website visits **by webpage**
- Profit **by customer**

Let's now talk about measures. These are arithmetic values for a row of data being analyzed. Examples would be:

- Sales in $
- Sales in units
- Returns in $
- Returns in units
- Cost
- Margin %
- Weight

- Units
- Visits
- Subscriptions
- Signups
- Downloads

We can do arithmetic on measures:

- Add
- Subtract
- Divide
- Multiply

For example

- Add sales of store A to store B
- Subtract sales this year from sales of last year
- Calculate average sale per customer
- Calculate profit margin

In most business data files, the number of dimensions will always be much higher than the number of measures. The most popular measures are sales in dollars, sales in units, and cost. The most popular dimensions are geographic (state, city, zip) or product dimensions (apparel versus shoes, men's versus women's versus children's), plus customer demographics such as age, income, and education.

Thus, the most popular combination for both dimensions and measures would be:

- Sales of shoes by gender
- Sales of jackets by state
- Total sales by city
- Total sales by age of customer
- Total sales by store

Last but not least is the type of business data called **time**. As we all know, 'Time is more important than money as you can get more money, but you cannot get more time'. *Jim Rohn*

Time is a very special and very important data item. There is no business analysis that excludes time. Time as a type of business data is a hybrid of measure and dimension.

It can be a measure when we:

- Calculate the difference in the number of hours being open over two days
- Calculate elapsed time between order and shipment

Time could be a dimension when we analyze:

- Sales by hour, day, month, quarter, year
- Profit by morning versus afternoon (such as in fast food restaurants)
- Number of units manufactured by minute

Gigantic Rubik's Cube

As you may have noticed, the number of combinations of all dimensions, measures, timeframes, customers, products, etc. could run into millions or billions.

If you have a thousand customers, twenty sales reps, and ten products and track sales daily, your database has 1,000 *20 * 10 * 365 = 73 million combinations to be analyzed, just for one year. Note that Amazon sells over 450,000 products and tracks sales by the hour. Walmart is not far behind. The average grocery store has over 40,000 products on its shelves at any given time.

So, let's imagine a gigantic virtual Rubik's cube—not with six sides, but with several hundred (one for each dimension). This is a good analogy to depict the complexity associated with marketing and sales analysis.

Thus, it is humanly impossible to analyze these amounts of data by hand or even in Excel. We have already discussed the market for analytical software, which is estimated at about ten billion dollars per year, just in the U.S.

Ways To Analyze Business Data

Let's assume that we have all the good quality data we need. It's easily accessible and ready to be analyzed. What do we do first? How do we prioritize our time?

In reality, businesses face many problems at the same time. Thus, the first task is to identify the largest problems as shown by the data. The second task is to prioritize them. The third task is to solve them. Let's concentrate on the first two tasks as we have already discussed challenges associated with the third; i.e., problem fixing that may not be in the analyst's control.

There are countless statistical algorithms, models, and methodologies to analyze data. You can get a PhD. in statistics or 'data science', as it is now called. Without discounting any of these approaches, I've found that the following three ways will answer over eighty percent of the most common business questions that can be answered with data. This is based on over twenty years working with global companies as well as mom and pop shops in many industries.

Pareto Or 80/20 Rule

The **Pareto rule,** also known as the **80/20 rule**, the **law of the vital few,** or the **principle of factor sparsity,** states that, for many events, roughly eighty percent of the effects come from twenty percent of the causes. Vilfredo Pareto (1848-1923), an Italian economist, first showed that approximately eighty percent of the land in Italy was owned by twenty percent of the population. Pareto developed the principle by observing that about twenty percent of the peapods in his garden contained eighty percent of the peas.

By applying this principle to business management , we find that, very often, eighty percent of sales come from twenty percent of the clients. Many other natural and business phenomena have been proven to exhibit such a distribution. The other business examples are:

- 80% of sales comes from 20% of products
- 80% of returns comes from 20% of products
- 80% of payroll is paid to 20% of employees
- 80% of costs are tied to 20% of products
- 80% of late projects are associated with 20% of all projects

Let's examine the significant business ramification of '80% of sales come from 20% of clients'. This means that we are dependent on a small number of customers for most of our sales. What would happen if we lost some among the top twenty percent? It may mean going out of business.

The next question is what percentage of profits these twenty percent of customers account for? We may be selling a lot to them, but not making a profit. If they account for more than eighty percent of profits, then the situation is even more serious and dangerous.

What if they only account for less than fifty percent of profits? Then we are losing money on some of them. Who are they? What would happen if we fired non-profitable customers?

The more customer/product combinations we have, the more important it is to know the distribution of risk or opportunity. After all, we are in the business of making a profit, not generating money-losing sales.

Part of the challenge is to know what the actual profit per customer is in the first place. And if you don't allocate the right costs of production, sales, and management to each product, you may be just flying by the seat of your pants all the way to the ground.

By the way, venture capital firms today refuse to fund a venture where a single customer accounts for more than twenty percent of sales. The concentration of risk is just too high. Too much is riding on just one customer—there is not enough diversification of business risk.

In summary, the 80/20 rule allows for a quick discovery of dependency on various business components such as clients, products, sales reps, and/or geographies such as cities or states.

Comparing the 80/20 rule to sales versus profits can reveal additional risks or lead to shedding the money-losing customers, products, or employees.

Growth

Let's say that we've examined our dependencies as described above. We found which customers make up twenty percent of sales.

Now the question is, which one is doing more or less business with us compared to last year (or any other time frame)? A year is the most popular comparison because it encompasses the full annual cycle of a fiscal year.

What if the number one customer on the list has purchased fifty percent less than last year? That would be adding insult to injury. Not only are we heavily dependent on them, but they are buying less from us.

How about other top customers? Are they buying less or more than last year? How about the profits? They may be buying less, but we may be selling them more-profitable items.

By now, you have a picture of how quickly we can identify two major problems; i.e., how dependent we are on a select group of key customers or products, and how that dependency is growing or shrinking.

Any management team worth their salt should know these figures and watch them very carefully, at least on a monthly basis. In my experience, less than twenty percent of businesses worldwide perform this analysis on a consistent basis. That's a lot of flying blind....

Would you invest in a business that does not do such an analysis periodically? The problem is that there is no way of knowing if such activities are taking place. What if they were?

Behavior Pattern Or Line Chart

The third question is how sales, profits, and costs 'behaved' over time. A pattern of decline or growth may be equally important to analyze.

Did sales drop in any particular timeframe in the past and are now steady? Or are they on a slippery downward slope for the last twelve months? The single best way to capture this metric is to display a line chart showing daily sales over the trailing twelve months.

How we are going to address these two problems may be very different. In the first case, it may have been a one-time occurrence that won't happen again because the one-time problem was fixed. But that may not be the case when we experience consistent erosion in sales over time.

Also, many businesses and/or products are seasonal and thus their sales are driven by weather, geography, or holiday shopping patterns, or all of the above. A good example is barbecue grills that may have different sales patterns in Minnesota versus Florida during the year (because it's hard to barbeque in Minneapolis when it's -30F in December), but spiking around the 4th of July in both states. Also, a lot of specialty product businesses experience seventy percent of their annual sales around Christmas.

In addition, displaying daily sales over twelve months may reveal temporary problems with logistics, poor service, natural disasters, etcetera—phenomena not accounted for by our marketing efforts.

We will demonstrate a report that combines all three components on one page. It's coming up in the chapter discussing visualization and storytelling.

The three ways of analyzing data are themselves a manifestation of the 80/20 rule. In this case, just three key data analysis techniques can provide eighty percent of the answers.

Mastering the application of these three basic techniques in the context of your business can lead to a significant improvement in your business operations. This does not mean that other analytical methodologies and techniques are of no relevance. It just means that the marginal utility of using them is less than the three basic ones.

The use of sophisticated statistical models is more relevant in physical processes such as manufacturing, transportation, or energy production. These processes depend much less on human preferences, tastes, and behaviors and more on scientific phenomena that can be much more easily measured and analyzed. At the risk of repetition, I want to stress that this book is devoted mostly to the analysis of marketing, sales, customer service and financial data—the bread and butter of any business of any size in any industry today.

Summary

Any business analysis needs to start with the analysis of changes in dependency over time. The most important task is to determine which disparity needs to be addressed first based on its size relative to the size of the business. If two are similarly sized (for example, the top two products each account for ten percent of total sales), the second criteria is the degree of change over time in sales or profits or both. The third is to determine if this change is due to one-time factors that are not relevant anymore, or whether they are the beginning of a favorable or negative trend.

I will demonstrate useful visualizations to analyze these problems with as few steps or clicks as possible. Such examples are coming up in the chapter on visualization and storytelling.

- How big?
- How did it change?
- Is the change a permanent trend?

8

Historical Versus Real Time Analysis

Rear View Mirror Versus Windshield

Traditional business analysis deals mostly with *post factum*, or historical data. We attempt to find answers to what happened yesterday, last week, month, quarter, year, or ten years ago.

The more time elapsed since the problem occurred, the less valuable the answer in terms of solving the underlying issue. This happens for several reasons:

1. We may not remember what happened in the past, even if it was just a week ago. We are all very busy and few of us have photographic memories of the details that may be necessary to explain a past failure. The more time that passes, and the more individuals that are involved, the less likely we will find the real answer and solve the problem. We may even have a wrong recollection of the actual events and not realize it. This is why we have a statute of limitations on certain legal proceedings.

2. It's water under the bridge. It happened, damage was done, we move on–as long as we don't repeat the same mistake.

3. It's too late to fix things that went wrong even if we wanted to. The circumstances have changed since then. For example, the incompetent person who got us in trouble has already been fired.

4. Getting all the information is time-consuming and financially prohibitive. We all have limited budgets and time and we have to prioritize the 'battles' we pick or problems worth solving. Digging into the past is very time consuming. The cost of getting an answer may exceed the value of the answer.

5. We can conveniently and convincingly blame them on past circumstances that were beyond our control—previous management, previous circumstances, lack of funds, change in customer preferences, natural disasters, etc.

6. The more time that has passed since the problem occurred, the less flexibility we have in fixing it, even if time or budget were not an issue. For example, the previous management team may have bought an expensive but not very good software product three years ago and we can't replace it in the next two years because we are bound by a long term contract.

Thus, the older the data, the less incentive there is on the part of managers to look back. Yes, you can learn something from it, but it doesn't help you that much today or in the future. This is a commonly held conviction among most managers. Also, most managers believe that the basic structure of business does not change daily and strategy is usually sound (otherwise they would be out of business), so historical data is of little value.

Most managers would rather work on problem prevention rather than fixing the failures of the past. Enter real time measurement and analysis...

Real Time Measurements

As we discussed, in most companies, business direction and performance is not going to change dramatically or immediately as a result of analyzing data from the past. Yes, we need to look in the rear view mirror from time to time, but it's much more important to keep an eye on the road ahead while racing against time and the competition.

In previous chapters, we discussed two major challenges faced by most companies: not knowing what you don't know, and a significant amount of time, money, and energy wasted on ineffective communication among employees. Business is a team sport, so the lack of communication and failure to work on the right problems may lead to expensive but otherwise avoidable disasters and headaches.

Given that employee cost is usually the single largest expense for many businesses, and that problems can only be solved by cooperating employees who know what needs to be fixed, it would be wise to address these two major problems at the same time.

The first component of such a solution (i.e., not knowing what you don't know) involves very detailed digital measurement of key processes in real time. Let's use a typical marketing campaign as an example. It's made up of at least ten concurrent processes:

1. Social media posts
2. Emailing
3. Online advertising
4. Website visits
5. Inbound and outbound phone calls
6. Online chats
7. Downloads of collateral materials
8. Orders
9. Payments
10. Shipments

The number of employees working on such an effort depends on the size of the company. Nevertheless, even in a small company, this is seldom handled by a single person because it's just impractical. The same principles will apply to construction, logistics, or manufacturing processes.

The first question is: Do you know which one of the ten processes is going as planned at any given point in time? First, did you set up KPIs for each one of them? Even if you did, can you monitor these ten

KPIs in real time? Ninety-nine percent of companies worldwide aren't doing this monitoring, so don't feel too bad about flying by the seat of your pants.

But you could do that if you had the right software platform with the right KPIs set up. The software required for this kind of monitoring exists already and may be cheap in comparison to the cost of not using it.

Real time reporting can alert you about process failures immediately if you set up the right KPI values. It's worth noting that if done right, the system will analyze the data automatically. For example, you may set up an alert that is sent simultaneously to three individuals responsible for the status of your website if your webpage is down or loading slower than expected. You may do the same for lower than expected visits, conversions, purchases, etc, etc.

Using Slack or MS Teams, you can set up alerts for relevant employees and notify them automatically about a problem that is happening now and could be addressed immediately. Since solving problems is a team sport as well, all employees could have their own individual problem-fixing checklists online relevant to their skills and responsibilities. They can easily update each other and management about the status of issue resolution. Every action of every employee could be time- and user ID-stamped. This increases transparency and accountability. In addition, such data can be used for *post factum* analysis of how the problem could have been avoided in the first place.

Such a process combined with employee monitoring is not very different from truck drivers who are being monitored by GPS using newly mandated systems for real time Internet tracking of their driving hours (they cannot drive more than ten hours per day, which they used to do). This is not very different from lawyers who log their time in 10-minute increments to respective clients. Nor is it very different from airline pilots who have been monitored in real time for quite some time now.

The trend toward accounting for every digital interaction is here to stay. It will find its way to all employees who work via keyboards, smartphones, tablets, or any digital device to perform their work (which most employees do). Tracking and analysis of actions in real time could be easy, fast, and cheap.

What *will* be hard is to define KPIs and the relevant levels of measures that trigger an automatic alert. What *will* be hard is to define who should know what when based on the problem at hand. By the way, don't count on Artificial Intelligence or Machine Learning to help you here. They are only as good as the rules you feed them. A process needs to be very well defined and broadly known before it can be subject to digitization, analysis, and automation.

But once it's done, you can put your process on autopilot and relax while flying at cruising altitude.

Killing Three Birds With One System

A system that automatically **measures** can also automatically **analyze** and **communicate.**
We have addressed the three single largest problems of an enterprise:

1. Not knowing what we do not know
2. Not being able to enforce quick action to fix a current problem
3. Spending too much time and money on ineffective communication among employees

In simple terms it can be stated that it's now possible to do the right thing at the right time at the right cost, thus preventing disaster or headaches or cost overruns in real time.

This would have been hard to imagine even ten years ago. However, due to the decrease in price of software to measure, analyze, and communicate, we should explore the value of real time data analysis and communication to significantly improve business operations.

The bottleneck is not the lack of software or the price of it. The bottleneck is the lack of knowledge that such systems exist or how to implement them. This is due to their novelty and the lack of prior experience to lean on.

Professionally and personally, I see a greater potential from real time measurement, analytics, and communication compared to traditional *post factum* business analysis. All companies need both functionalities, but the former has much greater potential to impact the bottom line.

Real time problem-solving stops problems from getting even bigger, too. It allows us to spot and address them at a fraction of the cost, especially if we factor in the substantial costs of communication problems and the resulting over-staffing. A quick reaction is becoming even more important in this age of short attention spans of most customers and their high expectations for problem-solving.

Actually, a good customer experience will be very hard to deliver without such a system. And customer experience is growing in importance as a marketing strategy. The problem is that the first good customer experience enjoyed by anyone anywhere defines their expectations for other businesses.

So, for example, if Amazon offers 1-Click checkout, the expectation bar for simplicity of the checkout process has just been set at one click. Next day delivery is already a virtual given. Easy and free returns are the norm. Full-time (365/24/7) live support on websites is nothing exceptional. Without a real time reaction system, it will get harder and harder to compete in the digital world of high customer expectations.

Thus, implementing such a system is not only important from a trouble-shooting or operational perspective. It becomes crucial from the strategic perspective as well. How much time you have to implement such a system depends on your industry as well as on your leadership vision.

- Quick Detection
- Quick Communication
- Quick Fix
- Quick Prevention
- Better Customer Experience

9

Visualization And Storytelling

A picture is worth a thousand words—yes, there is some truth to that statement.

One of the best examples of visualization of information comes from a French civil engineer, Charles Joseph Minard (1781-1870).

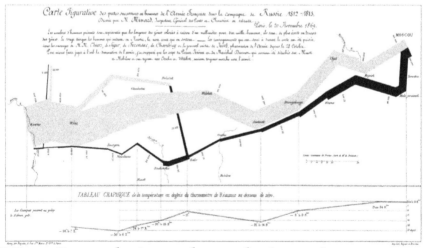

Minard's graph above shows the losses by Napoleon's army as they attempted to invade Russia in 1812.

The thick band at the top depicts the number of soldiers who crossed the border. As the army moved toward Moscow (from left to right in the graph) it experienced a loss of half of their soldiers as shown by the narrowing of the band approaching Moscow (*Moscou* in French).

As Napoleon's army retreated after the unsuccessful takeover attempt at Moscow, it had experienced further disastrous decimation due to a combination of low temperatures, poor supplies, and attacks from local Russian forces. The thickness of the lower, darker band shows how few soldiers survived the whole ordeal.

This picture shows six pieces of information at the same time:

1. The distance traveled
2. Temperature
3. Longitude
4. Latitude
5. Direction of travel
6. The size of the army

It's hard to imagine a better graphical depiction of a military campaign. By the way, the German army led by Hitler experienced an almost identical defeat about 130 years later. Those who do not know history, repeat the same mistakes. Invading Russia, a very large country, thus requiring very long supply lines, combined with very harsh winters is usually not a good idea.

As powerful an example as this is, it is inspirational only, because business today does not involve moving a lot of people around, and losing most of them due to warfare, starvation, and low temperatures. Nevertheless, it makes a point of displaying multiple measures and dimensions at the same time to illustrate the concept.

Powerful Visualizations

There have been many books and articles written on the best ways to show business data. There are many different ways to present information on graphs. All Business Intelligence vendors showcase colorful examples of graphs, visualizations, and dashboards. Just visiting their websites will give you an idea about the variety of ways to represent the data and information.

Presenting and discussing them here is beyond the scope of this book. However, following the 80/20 rule, let me share with you my three favorite ways to display a lot of information in the most simple way. With these three charts (or combination) you can illustrate eighty percent of business data.

Two Axes Graph

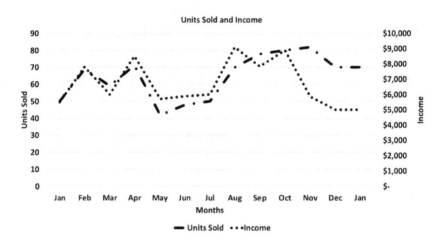

This chart shows the number of units sold by month for one year. At the beginning of the chart, in Jan and Feb, income went up at the same rate as sales. In Apr, income went up faster than sales. What may have happened? We may have sold more profitable products. That is usually a good sign. Profits grow faster than sales!

Let's now look at the end of year starting at Oct. Sales between Oct and Nov went up, but income dropped at a very significant rate. This is usually not a good sign. We are selling more units but making less money. The most likely scenario is that we're selling more of our low-profit products with lower margins, or that for some reason, our sales support costs went up.

And finally between Dec and Jan, our sales went down but profits were up.

This seemingly simple chart packs a lot of powerful information in it. Yet, without knowing the context of this business, there is no way to conclude if the trends are good, bad, or indifferent. Nevertheless, the chart serves as an early warning sign to take either corrective or supportive action, depending on the circumstances.

Double axis charts are perfect to compare two measures that have different units—in this case sales and income. It also works very well when one axis is in dollars and the other in percentages, such as percent of profit or returns.

Power Grid

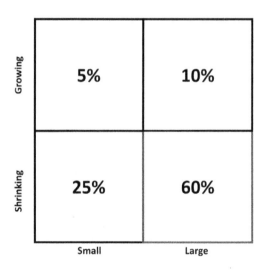

Let's imagine that we divided all our apparel sales into four buckets, and assume that we are comparing year-to-year data.

North West quadrant - five percent is the portion of all revenue from products that we sold more of, but they have a low price per unit. Think socks.

North East quadrant - ten percent of all our revenue came from products we sell more of and they have higher prices. Think dresses.

South East quadrant - sixty percent of our sales came from large items that we sold less of. Think men's suits.

South West quadrant - twenty-five percent of our revenues came from small products we sold less of. Think scarves.

This is not good news. Sixty percent of our revenue is associated with large products we sell less of.

In total, eighty-five percent of our revenue (60 + 25) is associated with products we sold less of compared to last year.

It's quite obvious that we should start our investigation with the South East quadrant by understanding what products make it up, and the trend of sales and costs like on the Two Axis Graph above.

Power Grid is probably the single most powerful depiction of possible problems in a single chart. It combines dependency with trend over time.

It can be produced for sales, or profits, or both. You may have KPIs associated with this graph; for example, the South East quadrant cannot exceed ten percent of sales.

When implementing Power Grid online, it's possible to make each quadrant clickable to other charts and figures. The most likely drill-down would be to the Two Axis Graph to find out if the changes are temporary or part of a trend.

When Power Grid is deployed online, it can be filtered for selected regions, products, or dimensions, thus enabling isolation of the single largest problem.

Every company in the world has the data to create Power Grids, yet too few use them in analysis.

Multi-Measure &Trend

	MTD	QTD	YTD	
LEADS	170	600	1,200	
NEW SALES	$12,000	$40,000	$60,000	
REPEAT SALES	$ 2,000	$ 40,000	$ 10,000	
TOTAL SALES	$ 14,000	$ 80,000	$ 72,000	

In sales and marketing analysis, it's important to analyze multiple timeframes and multiple categories at the same time. The single best analytical layout that is also easy to understand is displayed above. It's made up of categories lined up vertically with timeframes shown horizontally.

Let's discuss it from the analytical perspective. The first column shows four categories of marketing and sales:

Leads is the number of prospective customers that are interested but have not purchased yet. This is typical in long B2B sales cycles.

New Sales is the revenue from new customers that have never purchased from us before. The number of customers is shown below the dollar figure.

Repeat Sales is the revenue from additional purchases by existing customers. The number of customers is shown below the dollar figure.

Total Sales is just a sum of New Sales and Repeat Sales. The number of customers is shown below the dollar figure.

Thus, a sales manager can determine with a quick glance if business is coming from upselling or new customers, and if there are enough leads in the pipeline to sustain growth.

The columns show the figures for month, quarter, and year-to-date. The last column shows the revenue trend over the last six months.

Here again, a manager can see the relationship between each unit of time and quickly spot if they are going to make the final number and if not, which part they may need to concentrate on first. And here, again, without knowing the context of the business and the actual goals, it's impossible to conclude much from this standalone report.

Nevertheless, this simple report can reveal if we do not:

1. Do enough prospecting last month, quarter, or for a year
2. Acquire enough new customers for the same time frames
3. Do enough upselling to existing customers for the same time frames

Thus, this simple report can tell a lot about the nature of possible improvements or focus revisions. Do we need to concentrate on promotions, getting new sales, or upselling existing customers? These are the basic dilemmas of every sales manager.

The three ways to analyze data described above can meet a high percentage of the needs of any enterprise. This is especially true when such reports and charts are displayed online and can be clicked through or drilled down on to display the more granular underlying data.

Levels of Users

In most organizations there are three levels of users and needed skills.

The first is the analyst. This person needs to have access to granular data, be able to join or merge different data files, create graphs, sort, color-code, and perform statistical operations with the data at their disposal. Their job is to spot trends (good and bad), prepare and maintain ongoing reports, and answer ad-hoc analytical questions from management. This person is usually well trained in data analysis and can interpret data and information.

The second is the operations manager—in sales, finance, human resources, or marketing. Their job is not to analyze data but to keep the 'engine humming'; i.e., production lines going, bills paid, people hired, and products sold and promoted. They usually have KPI-driven goals and bonuses. Many were promoted from the ranks and have never taken a single course in analysis or critical thinking or technology. Most learned their skills on the job.

Yes, they need data, but they are seldom qualified or have time to analyze it. They need a roadmap or a GPS with a friendly voice warning them about road hazards and the estimated time of arrival; i.e., task completion. If there is a perfect analogy, it is a GPS or Waze indeed: tell me where to go, how to detour if necessary, warn me about hazards (accidents or weather) and provide an estimate of how much more driving I need to do and the estimated arrival time. And by the way, connect it to my calendar, so things are automated as much as possible and I don't even have to remember when to start driving.

It's easier said than done to deliver such functionality, but unless this is simple and relevant to the job, the information prepared by the analyst will just be ignored. In many cases, the operations manager will not even complain; their experience tells them that complaining to IT will not change much. They will pay lip service to analytics, but will not use it.

The good news is that the technology to deliver such a system already exists today. What may not exist is the vision and support from the top to implement such system.

The last but not least group of users is the executive. To use the car driving analogy, executives need not only a high level GPS, but fleet management software. They need to know at any time where their operation managers (vehicles) are at any time with respect to KPIs. They need to understand how the mix of their subordinates' performance impacts top-level company KPIs.

In addition, they need support to perform one-off, ad-hoc analyses to verify hypotheses about recently observed changes in the market. If market conditions change permanently, the new reality may need to be reflected through the KPIs of the whole organization. For example, if a competitor introduces cheaper products of equal quality but shorter delivery times, a team of top executives are responsible for defining the new driving speed and direction and/or detour.

Analytical and data skills among top executives generally are not strong, either. This is due to the fact that they became very successful without using data in general and have little knowledge and appreciation for the complexity of data-related issues at hand. Few top executives have a combination of digital technology, data, and strategy skills at the same time. This is especially true outside of technology companies. One great and telling exception is Sam Walton who brilliantly combined data, logistics, and retail to build Walmart into the behemoth it is today.

Therefore, the last two categories of users, operations managers and executives, need filtered, easy-to-access information that is relevant to the task at hand. Most have neither the time nor the skills—much less the desire—to analyze data as part of their job.

Visualization Is Not Enough

As discussed before, most people in executive suites and operations roles are not analytical. They need a simple, 'spoon-fed GPS' to navigate their business. It is also called storytelling. Let me share with you what I found while working with people in these roles.

For every manager with defined KPIs, an analyst prepares a PowerPoint presentation with no more than twenty slides (this can also be twenty screens, as long as it's easy to navigate through them). Analysts and managers jointly decide on the content of the presentation, with the analyst leading the effort by providing inspirational examples.

The presentation has the same structure every time it's generated (today most Business Intelligence vendors can automatically 'feed' PowerPoint slides with data from analytical databases). The same charts, graphs, colors, and fonts are used consistently.

The presentation starts with a high level summary and then breaks down the values of the top KPIs into its components. So, for example, if a manager is overseeing three states, then state-specific info is presented consistently in the same sequence.

In addition to graphs, PowerPoint provides automatic plain-English explanations of what the numbers mean. The idea is that a manager can print out a single slide (or export it to PDF) with a chart and numbers as well as a conclusion written on it. This single slide could be used in communication with concerned subordinates and business partners.

An in-depth discussion of the technical details of how to generate the automatic conclusions in plain

English is beyond the scope of this book, but it's discussed in depth during instructor-led workshops. (Contact information for consulting assistance is published at the end of this book.)

Nevertheless, here is an example of a Smart Slide with Smart Text.

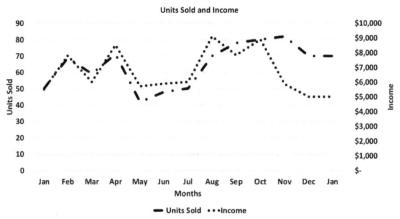

Between October and November income dropped sharply despite an increase in sales.

Summary

There are two major issues regarding data visualization:

1. Presenting the right amount of relevant information. Too many charts and graphs will just overwhelm and confuse most audiences.
2. Making sure that the information is understood by the targeted audience.

The first task is quite challenging by itself. The second is even harder. However, unless the information is conveyed via a standalone presentation or a single slide, it's unlikely it will be understood and acted upon. Thus, the whole effort to produce it will be wasted.

Unfortunately, this is not an uncommon occurrence today among companies large and small in all types of industries. Collectively, we have a lot to learn about how to analyze, present, and consume business information.

GREG GUTKOWSKI

10

Data Governance
And System Integration

In this chapter we'll discuss system integration. You may ask what this has to do with digital marketing. Why I should worry about it as a marketer? Isn't that the domain of Information Systems? Yes, and no. Marketing involves a lot of software tools that generate a lot of data that does not reside in one place, which makes it hard to analyze. Whether we like it or not, data analysis is the main driver of all of our efforts and if we can't analyze, we're back to the days of shooting from the hip.

Let me illustrate this challenging problem and opportunity from two perspectives: sales/marketing/financial and technology management perspective.

Let's start with taking a look at a day in the life of a B2B sales-professional who's trying to hit a sales target. Here are typical daily activities of a sales rep and software associated with those activities.

- When a sales rep makes a call, he will open a CRM to log the call there. The call can also be logged automatically by the phone system – IVR.

- When he takes notes he will do it in the CRM system.

- When he sends an email, it may be directly from Outlook or Gmail not necessarily integrated with CRM. That would be another system.

- When he wants to review a customer or a prospect web activities he'll have to visit social media sites, one at a time or look up at his Marketing Automation software or CRM, unlikely but possible.

- When he wants to engage in Twitter, LinkedIn, and Facebook to do posts, participate in discussions or groups he can use Marketing Automation software, but most likely he'll visit each media sites directly. To post a blog it's most likely he'll go directly to a blog site or use Marketing Automation software.

- To write a proposal he'll use a CRM or document management system or ERP. Most likely it'll be a word document stored on his hard drive.

- When he wants to review a status of an order, returns, sales volumes he'll use ERP.

- If he wants to look up status of an open ticket he'll use ERP or CRM or ticketing system.

- Finally, when he wants to take an order he'll log in to an ERP system.

As you can see the sales person will have to log in and log out to at least 6 separate systems during a day.

I know of no single company that offers a single, fully integrated system. Some CRMs are going this way but it's hard to have all the functionality in one system. Marketing automation systems concentrate on campaign management not on an individual prospect. The CRM vendors are trying to pick up a little more marketing automation functionality and Marketing Automation system are trying to pick up a little CRM functionality.

Today's reality is that there are multiple sign-ins. Even with a single password a sales rep has to use various systems. Often a sales professional integrates information by hand, looking up different systems one at a time.

Time spent on manual data integration is time not spent on selling.

Ask yourself – what percentage of sales professional time is spent on manual data integration instead of selling? Sometimes this number exceeds 50 percent. This means that we're paying a lot of money for clerical tasks done by sales professionals.

Now let's take a look from a technology management perspective.

In order to perform conclusive sales analysis, we need to integrate a lot of systems. Let's examine the types of information we need and the technical source for each of them.

- Basic customer demographics is stored in CRM systems such as saleforce.com, ACT, Sugar, etc.

- Notes on prospects and customers, copies of proposals can be stored in CRM or document management systems.

- Statistics on inbound and outbound calls can be stored in IVR, PBX, and CRM systems or can be tracked manually.

- Emails sent can be tracked by CRM and email systems.

- As far as social media activities, Twitter, LinkedIn, Facebook posts, discussions, engagements we'll have to tap to outside databases from social media sites through their APIs.

- Website customer visits data will come from Google Analytics or other web traffic analysis tools (sometimes homegrown systems). Other website activities such as downloads, signups, chats, purchases will be stored in Google Analytics.

- Orders, returns, sales volumes, and status of customer service tickets will be stored in ERP and ticket tracking systems.

The only solution to integrate all sales data is to put the relevant information into a single data warehouse. It is easier said than done for many reasons. And even if the data is integrated it may be

- Incomplete – lack of web activities for example
- Inaccurate – no all systems provide pristine data
- Not synced n time – dome data updated daily vs. weekly or monthly

So far, we've talked only about web traffic and sales analysis. Profitability analysis will require bringing in financial data, with all the challenges associated with it.

To provide campaign and/or customer profitability by product, geography, demographics, and time, we need to integrate data from at least Web analytics, ERP, and Accounting systems.

Return on Investment analysis brings about challenges associated with cost allocation. Are we looking at direct cost? Is the cost data fully loaded in to database? What's a definition of gross margin versus net margin? How do we define and allocate interdepartmental charges? A consistent ROI definition should be established and used for comparisons across the campaigns and over time. Otherwise it's like comparing apples and oranges.

There is a need for a strong partnership between IT and the marketing department. It's of paramount importance that these two departments work well with each other. They depend on each other more and more. Rapid technology changes impact the new ways to market, such as advertisements on smartphones. Traditional marketers are not technologists and they are not experienced data analysts. Traditional IT shops have a shortage of business data analysis skills. Computer programming skills are seldom compatible with data analysis skills. The conclusion: companies need to beef up their business analysis skills to bridge the IT—marketing gap. System integration is costly, but the lack of it is ultimately more expensive.

We need to integrate all of these systems to be able to perform real time analysis of our business efforts. Without such integration, we won't be able to take advantage of the latest and greatest digital technologies

Big Data Or Big Data Holes

Big Data and the accompanying Big Hype have puzzled me for quite a while, especially in the context of business analytics.

Big Data is supposed to be this Big Concept: we have lots of data, and even more data is coming at us faster than ever. The future of humanity hangs in the balance if we do not master it, understand it, and leverage it. In a nutshell, Big Data is a Big Deal. Is it really?

Big, more, and moving fast does not mean relevant, complete, sufficient, or necessary to analyze and help improve business performance. The avalanche analogy comes to mind.

A lot more granular data can indeed help in analyzing the economy, finance, climate, and other scientific research; but it has little to do with the analytical problems faced by most businesses around the world unless they are themselves in the business of science.

The rest of businesses (which is probably 99% worldwide by number) do not suffer from the Big Data challenge. I know of no business (outside of research) that is limited by the sheer amount of its own internal data. Computers today are powerful enough to handle most of the business data thrown at them.

But I know a lot of businesses that are very limited because the data they collect is either:

- incorrect
- incomplete
- inaccessible
- irrelevant
- not timely, or
- disjointed in silos of marketing, sales, production, customer support, and finance

Or some businesses just do not collect the data that could be relevant because it is:

- too expensive to collect, or
- too hard to analyze

The most common business analysis and data problem I've observed over the years is the tendency to generate separate Data Towers of Babel by marketing, sales, customer service, production, and finance teams—each in a distinctive language with no reliable translator on hand.

A great example is the Digital Marketing Tower of Babel. It is made up of 4 different incompatible data file formats for email, website ranking, paid online advertising, and social media marketing. In other words, we cannot even easily understand where our Internet leads are coming from. The problem is not Big Data or the lack thereof....

For the vast majority of businesses worldwide, the problem is somewhere else. It's the lack of technical and logical compatibility and the lack of translators between various business data files. It's data with Big Holes. As a result, it is hard to analyze what works inside our businesses and how to allocate operating capital among various marketing, sales, and service alternatives.

Thus, guessing substitutes for infeasible analysis. Energy is wasted and money drained down the data hole.

This is the problem that humongous armies of Accenture, IBM, and other system integrator consultants have been trying to solve for a long time for very large businesses for very large sums of money. They make gigantic Data Towers of Babel talk to each other for Fortune 1000 companies.

For smaller businesses, there was no hope until very recently. Collecting relevant data and then 'stitching it' across departments for the elimination of Data Towers of Babel was too expensive. Also, the technology to analyze data has been too costly and too hard to use for most.

No longer. With the advent of cloud-based software, cloud technology vendors decided to cooperate. The prices of software packages went down a lot as cloud vendors spread the development cost among many more users worldwide.

The cloud software vendors decided to speak the same language among themselves for the first time in the history of information technologies. The new language is called API, which stands for Application Programming Interface. It translates to a simple but powerful concept of various software packages 'talking' to each other in one common data exchange language.

For the record, API is not that new. What's new is the serious embrace of the concept by cloud software vendors worldwide. They've realized that no software vendor is powerful enough to impose its own language on everyone else. Until recently, the most powerful vendors have been jockeying for a position of dominance. No longer. They threw in the digital towel and started cooperating with each other and the smaller players using a common language of data exchange.

So now, one can stitch the 'best of breed' cloud software packages for marketing, sales tracking, dispatching systems, call centers, finance, and many others needed to run a business. This can be done at a very reasonable investment.

However, such integration is not very helpful without the tools to analyze all functions across the business. Fortunately for smaller businesses, analytical software packages also became very inexpensive. They are now much easier to use. And to share the analytical findings among all who need and care to know.

In conclusion, for most businesses, don't worry about Big Data. Worry about patching Big Holes—

left over of from numerous Data Towers of Babel still towering over your business.

The Achilles Heel Of AI Hype

There has been a lot of talk recently about the dangers of self-aware Artificial Intelligence (AI) robots replacing our jobs, killing innocent souls, ruining our planet, and finishing off our civilization. I am not sure how it may happen as AI is nothing but mathematical algorithms processing a bunch of 0s and 1s, and as such is incapable of ever thinking, reasoning, or threatening anyone.

AI is just a tech marketing term used to sell more software, hardware, services, and research around mathematical algorithms that have been around for years. The only new things are the increased computing power and more data that we can feed it. More power seldom makes things more intelligent.

More data may help, but that data needs to be relevant, timely, correct, and granular enough to make the whole concept work. The problem is that we lack the right data to explain most of the problems we are trying to solve today (despite collecting tons of data in general).

In meteorology, we cannot even predict the weather in our towns in the next 12 hours so we can leave our umbrellas behind. Why not? Because we do not have enough granular atmospheric data for our weather prediction models. Collecting relevant weather data is prohibitively expensive so our weather stations are sparsely located.

In medical research, we do not have enough granular, longitudinal, reliable, consistent, and clean data to learn what causes our bodies to stop producing insulin, or what causes most cancers or even a common flu. We don't even have a consistent medical patient records database to manage basic healthcare needs!

In business, 99% of companies have data in silos of marketing, sales, customer service, and finance not 'talking' to each other, which prevents us from the basic discovery of what really drives profits. Thus, a lot of resources are wasted on guesstimates. Case in point: it is almost impossible to attribute actual sales to most social media posts (not ads). The same is true with most radio, TV, and print advertising.

In economics, despite tons of data collected by the government and Wall Street, one can hardly spot down-cycles and warn the public about them. Remember the dot.com and 2008 crashes?

In politics, during the last U.S. elections, the media told us that one candidate had a more than 95% chance of winning just a few days before we learned otherwise. It was not the lack of computing power that led to such a conclusion.

We do well with algorithms when the data is clean, relevant, and plentiful. For example, computers can identify a malignant tumor from a high-resolution scan, but only because there are enough relevant pixels in the picture (computers are fed thousands of pictures with affected and healthy patient data so they can 'learn' from comparing the two sets). Yet, the same computer does not know what caused this tumor or how to cure it….as it lacks appropriate data in the first place.

In summary, we do not have the relevant data (granular, timely, and correct) to solve the majority of problems faced by humanity today, including healthcare, economy, weather, marketing, and politics.

Thus, the Achilles heel of AI hype is the lack of the right data. Despite lots of computing power and sophisticated data models. It's like driving a Tesla with no suspension.

11

How to Measure Your Business

So far, we've covered the basic concepts underlying business measurement and analytics.

Now it's time to get practical on where to start and how to make more profits using better measurement processes.

Every business large or small regardless of industry faces the challenge of resource allocation. No one can afford to do everything, and even if we could, the question remains—what should be the sequence of implementation? As we discussed, the measurement process is like a value-added chain, and a haphazard roll-out could derail the whole project. For example, it makes no sense to spend a lot of money on sophisticated analytical software if no one in the company trusts the underlying data.

Back to resource allocation: every business faces the question of where to focus first to increase profits the most. Typically there are three basic choices:

- Get more customers - impacts marketing and sales
- Sell more to existing customers - impacts sales and customer service
- Improve operations - optimizes existing processes such as design, production, fulfillment, supply chain, etc.

Let me illustrate with a simple example of a hypothetical company in the table below:

	Category	Before Improvement	After Improvement	% Change
1	New Leads	300	330	10%
2	Conversion Rate	20%	25%	25%
3	Customers	60	83	38%
4	# of Transactions	1	2	100%
5	Average Sale	$900	$1,200	33%
6	Total Revenues	$54,000	$198,000	267%
7	Profit Margin %	20%	25%	25%
8	Profit	$10,800	$49,500	358%

Let's examine this table. The first line is the number of sales leads our marketing department generated for our business. The second line is what percentage of these leads our salesforce converted to new customers. In this case, we brought in 60 customers (Line 3 Column A) when doing business as usual, and almost 83 after the improvement (Line 3 Column B). The number of customers went up almost 40 percent, but the two first measurements both grew less than that. Why did that happen? It's due to the cumulative effect of the process.

Let's continue at Line 4, # of Transactions. This reflects the number of products sold to new customers. In this case, we sold just one product before improvements and then we made sure to bundle other products for a total of 2. The next line is the average size of sale per product. We increased it by 33 percent; but line 6, Total Revenues, almost tripled (267 percent). Thus, we almost tripled our revenues without having to triple every category.

And this is not the end. Let's say we improved our internal operations by cutting unnecessary duplication or redundancies. Or margin went up from 20 to 25 percent (Line 7). Now our profit is up almost 4-fold!

In reality, each improvement for each line will cost time and money. Management needs to run this scenario and decide, based on their knowledge of the business, which category is the easiest to impact at the lowest cost. That would be the category to start with.

This framework can be used as a great communication and motivation mechanism. After all, here is a plan to improve profits 4-fold without having to improve all components four times!

Each category may require different data, processes, skills, and people for a successful implementation. It's a very different project to increase the number of leads and their conversion to sales as opposed to making operational improvements.

Nevertheless, it's the job of senior managers to decide on the appropriate allocation of resources based on business priorities.

Thus, the first step is to decide which category to start with based on cost and benefit. Regardless of the category selected, we will have to decide on more detailed supporting measures to be tracked and analyzed. For example, in the lead generation category, we may need to track the number of visits to the website, the number of emails sent and opened, as well as number of calls made. In operational improvements, the number of measurements to track and analyze can be quite extensive. Thus, we are back to the issue of setting KPIs, this time for each category.

Setting KPIs is one thing, but having the ability to track and analyze them will depend on the availability and quality of the data as well as the availability of analytical tools and skills to use them. Thus, the question arises: How can we measure our readiness with respect to these issues?

Let me introduce the Information Proficiency Test. It's based on the already familiar Measurement Value Chain framework discussed in Chapter 3.

The concept is rather simple but very powerful. For each of the selected KPIs, the following test is applied and scored on a 10-point scale:

1. Data Availability
2. Data Accuracy
3. Data Accessibility
4. Quality of Analytical Software Tools
5. Skills to Use the Analytical Software Tools
6. Readiness to Interpret information
7. Tools to Share Knowledge
8. KPI Quality

By scoring each KPI, it will become relatively easy to determine the weakest link in the information chain. It is also relatively easy to assess the investment needed to fix the weakest link. For example, if data accuracy is very weak, we can expect an expensive effort to fix the issue. On the other hand, purchasing the latest analytical software may not be a large expense.

Detailed scoring guidelines for each of the categories will follow at the end of this chapter. In the meantime, let me summarize.

A series of gradual improvements in key business categories can accumulate quite quickly. It is not necessary to improve all the components by the same rate to achieve a high overall rate of increase in performance. The trick is to determine which category is the least expensive and the easiest to improve, and what the sequence of the remaining improvements should be.

The cost of improvements may depend on the quality and the cost of getting and analyzing the underlying data. It's hard to assess such cost without a proven effective methodology that is easy to use and facilitates communication and managerial consensus among non-technical employees. The Information Proficiency Test provides such a framework. It allows us to assess and prioritize improvements in the underlying data structure, the 'oxygen' of all business operations. The quantity and the quality of the 'oxygen' will determine the potential for high performance—just like in athletics.

Information Proficiency Test Scoring Guidelines

Category 1
Availability of the Necessary Data

0 No data is collected to support a measure.

1-2 Some data is available from paper sources. Data cannot support the desired frequency of reporting.

3-4 Some data is available from paper sources and various electronic files on disjointed and incompatible systems.

5-6 All data is available from paper sources and various electronic files on disjointed and incompatible systems.

7-8 All data resides in multiple electronic files on disjointed and incompatible systems.
9-10 All data resides in one electronic, homogeneous database.

Category 2
Data Accuracy

0 Data has no technical integrity (incorrect representations such as data entry errors, multiple representations due to lack of uniqueness; e.g., multiple records for the same last name that is misspelled, wrong dates, etc.).

1-2 Data has some technical integrity problems. More time is spent on validating suspicious numbers than analyzing them. Management has realized that improvement is needed.

3-4 Data has no technical integrity problems, but common definitions are not established throughout the organization (e.g., how profit is defined, what algorithm is used to calculate ROA, or how new sales or cancellations are defined). More time is spent on validating the data due to the lack of common definitions than on analyzing the business meaning. Management has provided the resources to further improve data accuracy.

5-6 Data has no technical integrity problems and most definitions are documented. Some time is still spent on reconciliation due to various conflicting or unclear definitions.

7-8 Data has no technical integrity problems and all definitions are documented and communicated, but some managers question the definitions. Time is spent on discussions on what definitions would make the most business sense.

9-10 Data has technical integrity, all definitions are documented and clearly communicated, all managers support the definitions, and no time is spent on reconciliation of data.

Category 3
Data Accessibility

0 Data is not accessible from a desktop computer of any knowledge worker.

1-2 Some data is accessible to some knowledge workers from a desktop computer in the home office. Users do not have a readily available electronic list of all the data that could be accessed from their desktop. No field personnel can access the data. Networks are slow and not reliable all the time.

3-4 All data is accessible from a desktop computer of some knowledge workers in the home office. Some field personnel can access most of the data. Users do not have a readily available electronic list of all the data that could be accessed from their desktop. Reliability and speed of networks is still an issue.

5-6 All data is accessible from a desktop computer of some knowledge workers in the home office. All field personnel can access most of the data. Users have a limited list of all the data that could be accessed from their desktop. Navigation through available data is not user-friendly. Reliability and speed of networks is OK.

7-8 All the data is available to the whole organization based on a need-to-know basis. Networks are fast and reliable. A navigation scheme and list of available data is well documented.

9-10 All the data is available to the whole organization based on a need-to-know basis. Networks are fast and reliable. Remote access during travel is supported. A navigation scheme and list of available data is intuitive and flexible.

Category 4
Availability of Tools to Extract Information from the Data

0 No desktop tools are available to extract the meaning of the data. All managerial reports are on paper. Users have no tools for electronic manipulation of data.

1-2 Some electronic tools such as spreadsheets and databases are used by analysts. Re-keying information from existing paper reports takes up a lot of time. Use of graphs and/or statistical methods is rare. Turnaround time for reports requested from programmers is not satisfactory.

3-4 Only analysts use powerful but hard-to-use tools and provide the results of analysis exclusively on paper. Some managers use spreadsheets and databases to perform analysis for themselves. Re-keying of data is still being practiced.

5-6 Some managers have access to powerful tools that allow them to perform conclusive business analysis without assistance from an analyst. Re-keying of data is limited. Managers realized the need for more online management reporting and they are willing to use it to make decisions.

7-8 Most management reporting and analysis can be performed online either by managers or analysts. Almost no re-keying of data takes place. Most managers and analysts have flexible online tools that allow for identification and prioritization of quantifiable problems. Some statistical functions are available online.

9-10 All managers and analysts have flexible, intuitive, fast, and powerful online tools that allow for identification and prioritization of quantifiable problems. Answers to 80 percent of frequently-asked quantifiable business questions can be obtained directly from the screen in a numeric and graphical format with intuitive navigation that mimics the path of business analysis. The tools support exception reporting, 'what-if' analysis, forecasting, modeling, or any other relevant statistical need. Every tool allows the export and import of data to and from other tools.

Category 5
Readiness to Use Tools

0 There is no plan on how to train all the users on tools extracting information from data. Management does not support the need for training.

1-2 Training is delivered only if budget and time allows. If training plans exist, they are not documented. Some managers recognize the need for training.

3-4 There is a formal training system but it's not very well communicated and has a limited budget.

5-6 Training is planned annually for the whole organization. It's communicated and includes new hires and transfers.

7-8 Every user has been trained according to their on-the-job needs. Training plans and progress are monitored from time to time by senior managers.

9-10 Training effectiveness measurements are in place. Training plans and progress are monitored on an ongoing basis by all levels of management.

Category 6
Readiness to Use and Interpret Information

0 There is no plan on how to educate all the users on statistical, modeling, and information-interpreting techniques. Management does not support the need for such education.

1-2 Information interpretation education is delivered only if budget and time allows. If they exist, education plans are not documented. Some managers recognize the need for such education.

3-4 There is a formal education system but it's not very well communicated and has a limited budget.

5-6 Education is planned annually for the whole organization. It's communicated and includes new hires and transfers.

7-8 Every user has been educated or has plans to get information interpretation education according to their needs. Education plans and progress are monitored from time to time by senior managers.

9-10 Education effectiveness measurements are in place. Education plans and progress are monitored on an ongoing basis by all levels of management.

Category 7
Tools to Share Knowledge

0 All the knowledge is stored on paper and in the minds of users.

1-2 Some knowledge is stored electronically, but it's difficult to access due to the lack of a directory. Users cannot store their own knowledge.

3-4 Some knowledge is stored electronically and can be accessed relatively easy. Users can electronically store very limited amounts of knowledge and information for their own use, but their co-workers can't access it. Management recognizes the need for sharing tools.

5-6 Some knowledge is stored electronically and can be accessed relatively easy. Some users can share a limited body of knowledge. Management has committed resources to implement knowledge-sharing systems.

7-8 Sharing tools are being used by some departments. Users in these departments could not do their jobs without it.

9-10 Sharing tools are used throughout the whole organization, including senior management. Users have the ability to electronically add comments to screens, attach it to any number of relevant documents, and share it in an intuitive way with anybody they wish. Users have the ability to store knowledge by keyword in a combination of text, graphic, and voice formats and to retrieve it in the same fashion from any device, including smartphones.

Category 8
KPI Quality

0 No quantifiable performance goals are in place.

1-2 Some goals are defined, but there is no roadmap to achieve them. Few managers support the need to set goals and track performance.

3-4 Some goals are defined. Some managers have quantified their output, established measurements, and defined a way to achieve them.

5-6 Goals are defined and documented but not communicated throughout the organization. Progress toward quantifiable goals is reviewed on a regular basis by some managers.

7-8 All managers have established performance goals, documented a roadmap to achieve them, communicated them to subordinates, and review them on a regular basis.

9-10 Goals are established, documented, communicated, regularly reviewed, and tied to the personal compensation of managers and employees.

12

Summary and Call to Action

Let's summarize this book in the following bullet points:

1. More detailed measurement is now technically and financially feasible. This is a great opportunity to improve almost all aspects of running a business of any size in any industry. Until very recently, the measurement tools may have been cost prohibitive.
2. Potential is great but...it's not easy to decide what to measure because there may be a lot of new measures never used before. Even with the existing measures, it may be hard to decide what to measure more frequently and/or granularly; for example, consumption of electricity by a manufacturing machine every second, or conversion rates between various social media.
3. It's not easy to analyze the measurements. Conclusions need to be easy to understand, and most users are not analysts. Most

business users need to be 'spoon fed' with easy-to-understand conclusions and suggested next steps. Otherwise the whole analytical effort may go unused.

4. The existing data is unlikely to be in one place and may not be of good quality. To clean and organize data is expensive, unglamorous, and mundane. Yet, when it's not done, the lack of it is similar to broken plumbing. The data is like oxygen. We are unlikely to reach top performance with polluted lungs.

5. In business, there will be no perfect data ever. This is especially true in marketing because it's impossible to quantify the major drivers of the economy; i.e., consumer behavior, preferences, and tastes, as well as domestic and internal corporate politics. The right combination of data analytics and business experience will determine the success rate.

6. The importance of real time measurement and reaction is crucial for superior customer experience and not just operations. Today, especially in marketing, we need to move at the speed of opportunity as opposed to the speed of internal processes and politics.

Call to Action

Based on the Measurement Value Chain framework, wisdom is defined as acting on knowledge.

Implementation of the concepts discussed in this book may significantly increase the profitability of your business.

Such an implementation could be faster and more effective when assisted by an experienced executive consultant.

For a complementary 1-hour consultation:

Call 904.999.8826
Email info@3clicks.us
Or visit 3clicks.us

ABOUT THE AUTHOR

Greg Gutkowski, Digital Strategist & Bestselling Author has over 25 years of multidisciplinary global business experience spanning marketing, sales, and IT management, as well as Internet software development, IoT, advanced data analytics, and journalism. Greg has earned the following advanced degrees: MBA in IT Management, MS in Economics, MS in Journalism.

He currently runs the business analytics software company 3CLICKS.US and teaches business analytics and digital strategies at the University of North Florida Coggin College of Business.

Greg has worked over the years with customers from various industries. He has helped, among others: Allstate, American Express, Aon/Hewitt, AT Kearney, AT&T, Blue Cross Blue Shield of Illinois, Charmer-Sunbelt, Continental Bank, Dean Foods, Exxon-Mobil, First Bank, John Alden Life, Ralph Polo, United Stationers, and University of North Florida.

He has also designed analytics systems for several K-12 public and private school districts across the U.S. to assist them in evaluating the effectiveness of various education programs. His analytic software have been implemented by many leading U.S. school districts.

Connect with Greg on LinkedIn at
https://www.linkedin.com/in/greggutkowski

Other books by Greg available on Amazon:

1. Digital Business – How To Sharpen Your Executive Skills

2. Digital Tsunami – How To Thrive in the 21st Century

3. 9 Best Kept Secrets Of B2B Digital Marketing

CPSIA information can be obtained
at www.ICGtesting.com
Printed in the USA
LVHW051432160523
747134LV00013B/353

9 781724 820525